WHAT YOUR EXPLOSIVE CHILD IS TRYING TO TELL YOU

BOOKS BY DOUGLAS A. RILEY, Ed.D.

The Defiant Child
A Parent's Guide to Oppositional Defiant Disorder

The Depressed Child
A Parent's Guide for Rescuing Kids

What Your Explosive Child Is Trying to Tell You
Discovering the Pathways from Symptoms to Solutions

WHAT YOUR EXPLOSIVE CHILD IS TRYING TO TELL YOU

Discovering the Pathways from SYMPTOMS to SOLUTIONS

DOUGLAS A. RILEY, Ed.D.

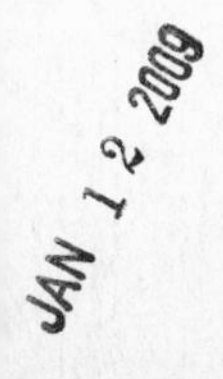

Houghton Mifflin Company
BOSTON • NEW YORK • 2008

www.houghtonmifflinbooks.com

Library of Congress Cataloging-in-Publication Data
Riley, Douglas.
What your explosive child is trying to tell you : discovering the pathways from symptoms to solutions / Douglas A. Riley.
p. cm.
Includes bibliographical references and index.
ISBN 978-0-618-70081-3
1. Behavior disorders in children—Popular works. 2. Temper tantrums in children—Popular works. I. Title.
[DNLM: 1. Child Behavior Disorders—prevention & control. 2. Child Behavior Disorders—psychology. WS 350.6 R573W 2008]
RJ506.B44R54 2008
618.92'89142—dc22 2008011841

Book design by Melissa Lotfy

Printed in the United States of America

VB 10 9 8 7 6 5 4 3 2 1

AUTHOR'S NOTE

None of the names or initials of the children and parents appearing in this book are real. Although it has been my great privilege to work with them, it is also my duty to protect their privacy. Because of this, various details have been changed or modified, and in some cases, composites of several children have been used. The case histories and anecdotes, however, provide highly realistic examples of the types of behavior that explosive children display and the issues that underlie their explosions.

To Debra,
by far my better half

CONTENTS

ACKNOWLEDGMENTS

MY UNDERSTANDING OF CHILDREN and their behavior is still a work in progress, even after nearly three decades in the psychologist's chair. I have learned from, and continue to learn from, a remarkable array of people over the years. It gives me great pleasure to thank them publicly and to say that I hope this book reflects on them positively and in a way that they would approve of.

The last year has seen the loss of two people central to my development as both a psychologist and a man. My dear friend Dr. Tom Lanning was very much the master of theory in counseling, psychotherapy, and personality testing. He had that daunting ability to read things once and grasp them in all their complexity. However, he much preferred to help others create insight into their lives through his piercing wit and spontaneity, and you could not leave an encounter with him without a smile on your face. Tom died on the evening of a blue moon, and like a blue moon he was rare, the kind of man who does not come along often.

Likewise, the passing of Dr. Robert Betz, professor emeritus in the Department of Counselor Education and Counseling Psychology at Western Michigan University, has left a void in my life, as well as in the lives of those who were lucky enough to have worked with him or to have been mentored by him in their professional lives. Dr. Betz was a professional baseball player, scholar, devoted husband and father, and genealogist, and his clear-headed, commonsense approach to counseling influenced hundreds of us during his long career. I like to believe that he would have read this book and found it to be useful to others, which would have been his highest compliment.

Having the opportunity to work with senior editors at Houghton Mifflin has been something that most writers dream about. Wendy Lazear invited me to join the Houghton Mifflin family (the sort of phone call that any writer would hope to get), and it was her careful guidance and review of my proposal when it was in its infancy that shaped this book into the form it takes today. Jane Rosenman saw me through the actual writing. Jane has ushered the writing of true luminaries to press, and her careful attention to my efforts caused me constantly to sharpen my writing as well as my thinking. I hope that the end result reflects well upon her trust in my ability to explain the behavior of children. Benjamin Steinberg, editorial assistant, kept the project on track, and Beth Burleigh Fuller and Barbara Jatkola, manuscript editor and copy editor, made sure that everything was tightened and honed. The final stages of turning the manuscript into an actual book and bringing it to market were ably handled by Susan Canavan, senior editor, and Elizabeth Lee, editorial assistant. While the flaws in this work are certainly mine, these dedicated professionals deserve credit for their individual and collective contributions to this book, and it is my pleasure to acknowledge them.

I have continued to receive the support and referrals of many pediatricians, nurses, teachers, and school counselors in my area over the years and remain flattered that they turn to me to help in the care and treatment of their patients and students. As always, I remain flattered by the trust that parents extend to me by asking me to work with their children. It is the children themselves who have been my real teachers, and I am thankful for all that they have taught me.

Lastly, and most importantly for me, I wish to thank my family. My sons, Collin and Sam, have grown into the kind of young men that I wish I had been at their ages. They are hard-working, energetic, creative, and giving, and it is my deepest desire, now that this project is finished, that they will still want to spend a few days with me in the mountains stalking trout and howling at the moon. My wife, Debra Lintz-Riley, is literally the foundation upon which this book has been built. She has put up with my long absences while researching and writing about the topics covered here. A remarkable observer of children, with an insatiable drive to get to the bottom of things, her insistence that I treat causes instead of symptoms has had a profound impact upon the way that I think about children and their behavior. I cannot thank her enough for her contributions and her forbearance.

It was six men of Indostan

To learning much inclined,

Who went to see the Elephant

(Though all of them were blind),

That each by observation

Might satisfy his mind.

—JOHN GODFREY SAXE
(1816–1887)

INTRODUCTION

THE OFFICIAL GOAL OF THIS BOOK is to help adults understand explosive children. But in truth it's not the adults I'm concerned with—it's the children.

There are important questions to consider. What must it feel like to be the child who is frequently out of control, and no one—parents, teachers, doctors—seems able to offer you the type of help that will allow you to enter into the good graces of others, every child's secret desire, because no one understands why you explode to begin with? As that child, what must it feel like to confront the stares—people always stare—on the faces of the children and adults who have watched you blow sky-high yet again, and know that they disapprove not only of what you have done, but also of who you have become? This is a fate that we hope to save our children from, and it is for these children that this book has been written.

Recall the blind men in the ancient Indian parable who were trying to describe the elephant: One, on touching the elephant's trunk, said it must be like a snake. Another, after placing his arms around its leg, said elephants must be like trees. And so on, each describing one aspect of the elephant's appearance correctly, and in doing so foolishly thinking he had captured the essence of its elephantness.

There is a similar narrow-minded tendency in the mental

health field today in which some writers think of explosive behavior as a "disorder" that can be treated using a single counseling technique, or a particular combination of medications. This one-size-fits-all approach may account for the increasing number of three-, four-, and five-year-olds who, after being kicked out of preschools and private schools because they are considered "bad" or "dangerous" are put on layers of medication in order to "cure" the explosions. After thirty years of working with these children, who, I might add, are as sweet and loving as any other child except during their explosions, it is clear to me that they deserve the same level of effort we place on trying to understand physically ill children or children who are suffering from depression or anxiety.

While the one-size-fits-all approach to explosive behavior is seductive and inviting, it is ultimately wrong, because, like the blind men, it fails to see the larger picture. The larger picture is this: Explosive behavior, as loud and uncomfortable as it is to witness or live with, is not even the real problem. Rather, explosive behavior is simply a symptom of the hidden but very real issues that a child is struggling with deep inside.

These issues can seem immensely varied and confusing until you know what to look for. But, once you have this knowledge, the treatment for each can be quite straightforward. In this book I cover the most common reasons children explode, as well as the not so common reasons. And just as important, I provide real strategies that are designed to work with the underlying causes of your child's explosions.

So, our main task as parents of explosive children or as professionals who treat them is to expand our viewpoints in ways that allow us to recognize the issues that are working in the background of a child's life. An example might serve to illustrate where we are headed: Some children seem to be born with the type of personality that makes it almost impossible for them to gracefully accept unexpected transitions or changes in their schedule. Few people witnessing the explosions would know that their brains automatically process unexpected events or transitions ("pop-ups," as one child calls them) as serious danger signals, and this is why they fight and argue, or go on red alert when faced with an unexpected event that other children get through easily. For such children, explosions have nothing to do with being oppositional or willful or bratty, the conventional explanations. Rather, they are so sensitive to unexpected events that they literally explode with anxiety when faced with one. Should you continue to read, you will soon find out how to use commonsense methods to treat this, as well as the other underlying causes of explosive behavior. My hope is that you will ultimately come to see explosive children as the remarkably complex little human beings that they are, who are nevertheless capable of being treated and cured through kindness and love, and without resorting to the use of force or multiple medications.

What is your explosive child trying to tell you? Without realizing it, they are saying through their actions that something deeper is going on, something that deserves your attention. You must remain aware that young children do not have the vocabulary or the verbal skills to tell you what is bothering them or discomforting them, and that their moods and behaviors are the language that you will have to learn to decipher in order to hear them out.

While this book is about children in the roughly three- to ten-year-old range, it is my belief that older children, and even adults, likewise stand to improve their lives once they begin to analyze their own explosions. I have had a great number of parents who, once we begin to talk about the hidden reasons that children explode, say to me, "That sounds like his teenage brother," or "That sounds like me." It is in this regard that I hope interested readers will take the ideas presented in this book and apply them even more broadly than I had originally planned. It makes sense, once you consider it, that analyzing why children explode may have a great deal to tell us about why teenagers and adults explode. My hope, obviously, is to bring to a halt a child's explosions while he or she is still young, so that the teenage and adult years can be happy, peaceful, and productive.

WHAT YOUR EXPLOSIVE CHILD IS TRYING TO TELL YOU

1

I AM NOT A BRAT, JUST A CHILD WHO NEEDS HELP

IMAGINE THE CHILD you see at the supermarket, the one who makes you want to drop to your knees and shout out loud, "Thank God he's not mine!" We're talking about the hitter, the kicker, the spitter, the fit thrower, the screamer, the child who attacks parent and peer with so little provocation that you can't help but ask if he is possessed. The problem comes when you can't just walk away, privately shaking your head and wondering where his parents went wrong, because *you* are the parent, he is *your* child, and he's going home with *you*—just as soon as you can drag him out to the car and find a way to keep him buckled in. What is a parent to do?

Why Does My Kid Act Like This?

When parents call my office to make an appointment for a child who is about to get kicked out of kindergarten, or a child who has brought them to within half an inch of social isolation from neighbors and friends because of behavior problems, they have one thing on their minds: "Why does my kid act like this?"

Parents — mothers in particular — are natural scientists when it comes to this question. They spend hours developing hypotheses about why their child acts the way he does, pondering and worrying themselves sick. What mother, way down inside, doesn't suspect that her exploding, tantrum-throwing, melting-down child is just a brat? But if you are one of those moms or dads whose child's tantrums are the stuff of kindergarten legend, simply labeling him as a brat does nothing to quiet those nagging suspicions that something deeper is going on. The problem with the "B" word is that it fails to tell you *why.*

That *why* is the itch that has to be scratched if you are to come to a true understanding of how to help your child. As you will soon learn, the answer to why children explode is far more interesting, and far more complex, than the brat hypothesis.

The first step toward arriving at *why* is to come to an understanding of the different types of explosions that children display. While most dramatic tantrums may look and sound pretty much the same to the overwhelmed parent who is standing there watching, all explosions are not created equal. I will demonstrate this to you briefly. Before I do, though, I want to ask you to do your best to avoid falling into either of two traps. The first one is confusing symptoms with causes. When working with children who explode, you might be tempted to think that the explosions are the problem, or, in medical terms, the *disorder.* Common sense should tell you, however, that children do not sit happily playing and then *Bang!* explode for no reason. There is something hidden, something working beneath the surface that sets them off time after time.

The second trap is lumping all of the possible causes of childhood explosions into one heap and claiming that there is a universal technique that can be used to treat them. Such thinking is like saying that a pain in your head must be caused by the same problem as a pain in your leg, your stomach, or your shoulder and that all of them can be treated with an aspirin.

Steven and Henry

Think of explosive outbursts as icebergs. The observable part, that one-tenth that sticks up above the surface, is the yelling and screaming, the bulging eyes and flailing arms, the spitting and kicking and cursing that exploding kids let fly in the midst of their fits. The nine-tenths that we can't readily see are the actual causes of the explosions. This is where we become detectives, entering into the mystery of incredibly powerful forces.

Once you learn to consider all of these forces, you will begin to understand why your child is responding to the world in a very specific manner and the blowups will begin to make sense to you. This is not to suggest that you will like or condone your child's explosive behavior. You will, however, understand what makes it happen and be more able to respond in a way that will decrease the explosions.

The following two examples will show precisely why the iceberg analogy is useful. Steven and Henry were both first graders, and both were assaulting their peers. Steven did it at the bus stop. Henry did it mainly in the school cafeteria, but also sometimes in the hallways or in the school library. Before coming to my office, the parents of both children had tried time-outs, loss of privileges, rewards, and talking/lecturing/yelling/spanking/bargaining/bribing/counting, all to no avail. The assaults simply continued. Both boys were in danger of being placed into alternative educational settings. Their schools and other parents had begun to label them as oppositional and explosive and were demanding that something be done quickly.

Steven would strike most parents on first glance as quiet (mousy actually), anxious, and certainly not prone to display the in-your-face, coequal-with-the-parent attitude typically seen in oppositional children and adolescents. At the bus stop, though, he would climb onto the backs of the other children and pull their hair, or pull them backward off the steps of the bus by their coats or belts.

On one occasion, he clawed a child's face so badly that she had to be taken to the doctor's office.

Henry, by contrast, was a beefy little guy with a chronic frown. It was easy to believe that he could be an angry actor. His method of assault was more straightforward than Steven's. He would punch the kid he was mad at right in the face. Being roughly a third bigger than most of his peers, he could do a lot of damage.

What I found when I got to know Steven better was that his thinking had a marked obsessive streak. He had developed the belief that he *had* to be the first one on the bus every day. As he walked to the bus stop with his mother, he would begin to whine anxiously if he saw that another child had arrived there before him.

The battle that his mother fought with him every morning was precisely the opposite of what goes on in most homes. Most kids have to be threatened to leave in time so as not to miss the bus. Steven would have gladly left an hour early if his mother had been willing to put up with it, and his need to get there first created tension at the breakfast table every morning. Steven believed that he had to be the first one on the bus in the same way that you or I believe that we have to breathe air. The power of this belief caused him to assault any child who tried to get on before him. From his viewpoint, being first was a life-and-death issue.

Now, back to our friend Henry. He had what is referred to as sensory processing disorder. He wasn't a worrier and he wasn't compulsive in any manner. Instead, he had an exquisite sensitivity to touch or pressure. Tags in his shirts bothered him horribly, and when he was younger, he was guaranteed to pitch a world-class fit if the toe seams of his socks were not lined up just so. He always complained that his clothes were too tight. He would stretch the necks of his T-shirts out so far that they would almost slip over his shoulder. Along with all of this came an exaggerated need for personal body space, because anyone brushing against him, even lightly, sent him into orbit.

The bane of children like Henry is the fact that young kids

spend lots of time standing in line at school. When other children bumped into him or rubbed against him, he felt assaulted. He hit back out of what seemed to him to be self-defense. The chronic frown on his face was there because he believed he lived in a world in which he was constantly being attacked by others.

By identifying the causes of each boy's meltdowns, the solutions became clear, and I am happy to report that Steven and Henry and their parents are now all doing quite well. But it wasn't without some initial head-scratching about the causes of their behavior.

A Taxonomy of Tantrums

All kids have tantrums, meltdowns, and explosions. It is simply part of being a kid. Some of these tantrums and meltdowns come under a heading that I use frequently: painfully normal. What parent hasn't had the experience of dragging a child out of a store, the child engulfed in tears and rage over not getting some particular toy? Incidents like this mean nothing about a child's psychological operations, other than that they are normal.

Tantrums, meltdowns, and explosions rightfully become a concern, however, when your child takes them much further than other kids. You are correct to worry when you realize that your child is a powder keg compared to his or her peers. At some point, if it becomes clear to you—in the comments you hear from relatives or neighbors or your child's teachers, or in the way other kids avoid your child—that something is not right, you need to take action.

In this book, I will ignore the painfully normal fits and tantrums that every child experiences, because with time and maturity, they simply go away. Instead, in each of the following chapters, I will focus on the causes and appropriate treatment of these tantrums and explosions that are sure to be detrimental to your child's happiness and success.

I believe that the primary cause of highly explosive behavior in children (and frankly, even in adults, which makes it all the more important for your child to receive treatment early in life) is what I refer to as *road map meltdowns.* Explosive children are prone to make assumptions about what is going to happen in the near future. These assumptions — their mental road maps of the future — can be like little "movies" of what they think is going to happen next. Road maps get elevated in their minds to the status of 100 percent certain, totally gonna happen probabilities. When what the child believes is about to happen does not come to pass, his road map disintegrates. Parents who say that their child behaves as if his world has ended because they stopped at the drugstore when the child thought they were going straight to the grocery store do not understand just how right they are. When a child's road map does not come true, his world *does* cease to exist for a few moments. The resulting dramatic tantrum shows us how overwhelmed some children can become when faced with anything unexpected. I will say much more about this issue in chapter 2.

There is also the issue of defiant behavior versus explosive behavior. I find that there is an alarming confusion among parents, teachers, and others who work with children about the terms "defiant child" and "explosive child," in that they believe these terms to be interchangeable — just different words for the same behavior. In reality, these are two distinct sets of issues. While it is true that children who are "defiant" can be explosive, and children who are "explosive" can be defiant, the underlying personality characteristics of the two groups are entirely different and require different treatments.

In my experience, most explosive children — the ones throwing punches in kindergarten or the ones who get down on the floor and throw massive fits — tend to suffer from the road map meltdowns just noted above. The truth is that their explosive behavior can also be caused by any of the issues that are discussed in this book.

Defiant children (also referred to as "oppositional children") aren't particularly nervous or anxious, and aren't particularly bothered by unexpected changes or events unless they prevent them from doing something they were strongly looking forward to, much as any of us would be. Instead, defiant children are exquisitely sensitive to the issue of power—who has it, how much they have, and how to demonstrate that no one can make them do anything. From a remarkably early age, they do not like to be told to do anything by anyone. They act the way they do in an attempt to pull equal with their parents and other adults regarding power and influence.

Another prime cause of explosive behavior has both nothing and everything to do with psychology. In chapter 3, I go to some length to discuss the part that allergies and food sensitivities can play in childhood explosive behavior, particularly in the age group I concentrate on in this book—three- to ten-year-olds. The fact that we rarely think about allergies and food sensitivities in relation to behavior tells us just how shortsighted we have become. Parents and professionals alike are apt to launch into complex behavior modification programs or commit to long-term use of mood-stabilizing medications before considering the simple notion that what children eat or drink or breathe just might be having an impact upon their behavior. Allergies and food sensitivities must be ruled out if the true desire is to treat causes, not symptoms.

There is considerable dissension even among allergists over this issue. Suffice it to say that over the years, I have become keenly aware that a remarkable number of the exploding, irritable children who get referred to my office for behavioral treatment have bags or circles under their eyes, ruddy ears or cheeks, a chronic runny nose, a history of ear infections, or a history of bouncing off the walls after consuming certain foods or food additives. I am also too aware of the children I see who have been given diagnoses as serious as bipolar disorder, only to have their symptoms greatly diminished after being treated for allergies or food sensitivities.

• • •

There are other equally important issues that we should not ignore regarding explosive behavior. For example, two of the causes of explosive behavior are generalized anxiety disorder and depression. Anxious or depressed children are not just miniature versions of anxious or depressed adults. They act differently. In fact, cranky, explosive behavior can be one of the main symptoms that alert us to these underlying issues of anxiety and depression.

There is also the issue of childhood bipolar disorder, which is discussed briefly in chapter 8. Children who suffer from it can be notoriously volatile and unpredictable. There remains, however, considerable disagreement about whether this diagnosis should even be used with young children. Some of this disagreement revolves around the absence of observable periods of manic behavior in children, believed by some theorists to be one of the symptoms necessary to make such a diagnosis. Others argue that edgy, agitated, explosive behavior is the leading edge of childhood bipolar disorder, a predictor of what is to come. It is a difficult diagnostic call to make, because bipolar disorder seems to unfold over time. Its symptoms emerge gradually, until finally it becomes obvious that bipolar disorder is indeed the correct diagnosis. Along the way, bipolar children are almost invariably misdiagnosed as being depressed or as having attention deficit hyperactivity disorder (ADHD) or oppositional defiant disorder. No doctor has a crystal ball, yet I find that today many try to diagnose bipolar disorder too early, and use medication to treat it before fully exploring other causes.

What about the relationship between attention deficit hyperactivity disorder and explosive behavior? Children who have ADHD, though often highly creative and imaginative, can be disruptive to an entire classroom, and their impulsivity and inability to anticipate the consequences of their behavior often leads to explosions and altercations with adults.

There is growing evidence that sleep problems and sleep-disordered breathing can result in explosive behavior, and children with these problems frequently get misdiagnosed as having psychological issues. Sometimes, simply having tonsils and/or adenoids removed can make all the difference in how a child behaves.

Maturity also plays a role in explosive behavior. It is a mistake to believe that a child's intellectual development and emotional development unfold at the same pace. Yet how often have you heard an adult say about a child, "She's so smart. Doesn't she know how to act better than that?" Emotionally immature children explode for reasons that have nothing to do with being oppositional and little to do with road maps. Their treatment needs to revolve heavily around learning social skills, to a degree that is quite different from the needs of other exploding children.

Children with an expressive language delay, a different sort of developmental issue, are easily frustrated by their inability to communicate with others. They are often pointers and grunters during their early lives and can be explosive when you fail to understand what they are attempting to communicate to you. Children with language delays are known to have more problematic behavior than children without language issues.

Children with learning disabilities and processing issues can become immensely frustrated with their inability to master classroom tasks that they see their friends mastering with apparent ease. Often thought of as explosive, oppositional, or defiant when they refuse to take part in classroom activities, they are really just attempting to protect their own dignity by not publicly exposing their academic weaknesses.

Sometimes it is more important to be concerned about what the world has done to an explosive child than about what the child has done to the world. Children's explosions may be related to bullying, family instability, negative parenting practices, and the like. None of us should be surprised by how a child acts when he has lost his sense of safety, when the frustrations of an unsafe world become just too much to tolerate.

Why Ask Why?

There is compelling evidence that we are playing for large stakes, that we must find and treat the causes of explosive behavior early in a child's life in order to prevent lifelong problems. One study of individuals who were followed from birth until around the age of forty found that the lives of ill-tempered boys, in comparison to their more even-tempered peers, were marked by lower levels of work success and career satisfaction, lower rank in the military, and higher unemployment rates. Ill-tempered girls tend to marry less successful men, and ultimately became ill-tempered women and mothers.

Given how varied the causes of childhood explosive behavior are, we should never again be tempted to think of a child's explosions in simple terms. In this book, I delve deeply into the lives of children to find what is not easily seen — the causes of their explosions — in an attempt to free them from a downward spiral. The good news is that after parents uncover the factors affecting their child, the fixes are often quite straightforward. This will become clear as I dissect explosions into their many forms and causes, as I did earlier with Steven and Henry. Eskimos are said to have many different words for the concept of "snow," as do the Irish for the concept of "green." We must develop the same mindset to truly understand the meaning of the word "explosion."

People frequently ask me why I am so fascinated by explosive children. If I survey my career, I realize that explosive children have always been the ones who have puzzled me the most. Like those parents I spoke of earlier, I want to know *why.* If my almost thirty years of working with children have taught me anything, it is that there will never be a simple explanation for why children explode. The causes of their explosions, mostly hidden, are exceptionally varied and come from all over the medical and psychological map. But we live in a society that often sees these children in simple terms and does not acknowledge the complexity of their struggles.

No child should end up stigmatized and rejected, particularly for the hidden causes of explosive behavior that we will explore. You will quickly learn that the forces behind a child's explosive behavior are so strong that your help and insight will be needed in order to help the child gain control. In addition, you will soon become much more sympathetic in your view of what any explosive child is going through.

No parent wishes to measure his or her family's happiness by how long it has been since the last explosion. Neither does the child, whether she is three or eight or ten or even older. This child, like most children, is desperate to earn praise and acceptance. Children who have massive blowups do not like the way they feel after they erupt. They end up in trouble at home and at school, and their peers begin to avoid them. When all is said and done, they begin not to like the lives they are leading. There is no more compelling reason than this to begin your search for the hidden cause of your child's explosions.

2

CHANGES AND TRANSITIONS MAKE ME EXPLODE

*

IF YOU REALLY WANT to understand massive explosions—the ones that leave a crater where your living room used to be—you have to come to terms with the idea of mental road maps. Mental road maps? We all have one. It is your mind's private image of what you think is going to happen, something like a little movie that shows you step by step what your day will be like. My road map of a typical weekday morning has me leaving home around 7:20 A.M. and heading down Highway 17 toward my office. I'll stop at a certain store to get my newspaper and something to drink. After that, I will drive to my office, go in and water my plants, listen to my messages, and get ready to see my first patient.

I have done this routine many times, and usually things go as expected. If the store is out of Diet Dr Pepper or *USA Today,* I'll be irritated, because I don't like to make do with the other brands. But I'll roll with it easily enough, unlike the guy I saw yelling at the clerk: "I *always* get my newspaper here! You have it *every* day! How could you possibly be *out*?"

While I certainly hope to make it the rest of the way to my office without incident or surprise, if I get a flat tire, I will find somewhere to pull over and change it. I'll mutter a few choice words while I'm at it, but by the time I get to work, I'll be fine. My job, as I see it, is to deal with disruptions in my expectations sanely and efficiently.

This touches on a significant aspect of road maps — their tightness. I have a relatively loose road map, one with only a few details and expectations filled in. Some people, however, have tightly knit road maps filled with many details and expectations. They have an unusually strong need to know what is going to happen, because not knowing creates anxiety. This drives them to make predictions, which in turn fills in their road map and makes them feel safe. They take these predictions to the extreme, convincing themselves that what they want to happen or think is going to happen is the only thing that actually will happen. Having to deal with the store being out of their favorite newspaper or beverage might reverberate in a negative manner throughout the morning. A flat tire can wreck the entire day.

These people can come across as rigid and unyielding when asked to do something unexpected or different from what they had scheduled. If you doubt this, take over the scheduling at my office for a few days: "No, I can't bring him on Tuesday night because that's when my favorite TV show comes on. I can't miss my favorite show."

Road maps have other purposes, too. For one, they help us to remain happy and optimistic by keeping in conscious thought the more enjoyable things that can happen and excluding from conscious thought the most worrisome possibilities. This is very important, because it gives us the illusion of safety. When you think about it philosophically, how can any of us leave the safety of our homes and venture out into a world in which we know bad things can happen? As Dorothy and her companions in *The Wizard of Oz* lament, "Lions and tigers and bears! Oh, my!"

The Big White Room

Given all of this, allow me to state an opinion about why children with road map issues explode: Children need to feel safe, and one of the ways they make themselves feel safe is by generating predictions about the future. When a child's predictions don't come true, we have a situation that is ripe for a road map meltdown, the point at which a child's predictions collide with a reality that is far different from his expectations.

What effect must it have on a child when his predictions come out so totally wrong? Most children can't explain what the loss of predictability does to them psychologically. A mother I once knew taught me an important lesson about this by introducing me to the concept of The Big White Room.

She was the mother of a boy I was seeing for counseling. She called me on a Friday, saying that she had a personal emergency and had to talk. When we sat down, I asked her to tell me what was going on. She said that several things had happened that morning. Her husband of fifteen years had come home earlier than usual, which made her fear that he had lost his job. He had not. He said that he had come home because there were a number of things he had to tell her. First, he told her that he was not happy in their marriage and that he was leaving. Second, he told her that not only was he leaving, but he was leaving that weekend. Third, not only was he leaving that weekend, but he was moving in with another woman. Fourth, not only was he moving in with another woman, but the woman was pregnant with his child. Finally, not only was she pregnant with his child, but she would be delivering in two months.

I asked her the question that all psychologists ask in such situations, which in retrospect seems pretty stupid and obvious: "How do you feel about that?"

"I'm in The Big White Room," she answered, shaking her head in disbelief. And then she proceeded to tell me that her entire world had fallen away, just disappeared, and she was left standing alone in a space that had a shiny white linoleum floor that stretched to infinity on all sides. There was no ceiling and no visible walls, only the infinite floor. No furniture. No people. Everything that had earlier in the day constituted her world was gone.

She told me that it was the most frightening feeling imaginable and she felt so frozen with fear that taking even one step in any direction would cause her to lose her mind.

I want you to think about what the crashing down of expectations and comforting predictions about the future did to this highly intelligent mother of three, how it rattled her sense of safety and understandably so. Some children, the ones who have road map issues, seem to feel as if they have been transported to The Big White Room by even the most minor disruptions of life. The overwhelming emotions that occur at the moment of a road map failure are just too much for them to contain. That is why they explode.

A boy I once worked with, whose family called him "Tyler 2" to distinguish him from his father, "Tyler Senior," explained why he melted down over such seemingly small events as his mother stopping at a store he had not expected her to stop at: "Surprises like that are small, but because they are so random, they feel really big." His belief in his road map was so strong that even a small deviation felt like something "random" and "big"—and, needless to say, negative. Moments like this caused him to ignite, and off he would go.

Lee is a kindergartner who could be described as generally happy until confronted with something he has not anticipated. He was cruising along as happy as a clam for the first week of school because his best friend would stand at the main entrance and wait for him every morning. While his mother was pleased that his school year was getting off to such a good start, she was also on pins and needles because she knew from experience that Lee was a meltdown waiting to happen (her description, not mine). She tried to tell him that his friend might not be able to wait for him every morning, but he more than insisted that she was wrong: "No, Mom! You don't know! You shut up!" Her saying such things tampered with his road map and drove his anxiety level up, reminding us that anxiety is the trapdoor to anger: he was prone to let his mother have it when he was anxious or uncomfortable. Then one day his friend was not there. Spontaneous combustion! Road map meltdown, right there in the car! Kicking and screaming and whacking everything in sight, Mom included. Lee was, according to his mother, absolutely inconsolable all morning and not in any way fit to go to school.

Why Some Children Explode and Others Don't

To bore a bit deeper into it, why do some children, such as Lee, explode and others don't? Everybody has a road map, but not everyone melts down when his or her predictions don't pan out.

There is ample reason to think that the way we react to the world may be hardwired into our brains by the time we are born. In one experiment, infants with higher levels of electrical activity in the right hemisphere than in the left became inhibited and withdrawn when faced with a situation they had never encountered before. Infants who had the opposite pattern were less withdrawn or inhibited. Interestingly, inhibited children who became less inhibited over time tended to show a shift in brain wave pattern to the left hemisphere.

Neuroscientists have also studied other areas of the brain in a search for clues about our behavior. Of particular interest is the amygdala, the almond-shaped bundle of neurons at the base of the brain that triggers strong reactions to new or unexpected situations by flooding the upper, "thinking" parts of the brain with signals to fight, flee, or freeze. The tendency in infants and children to experience strong emotions and not to do well when faced with a novel situation is called behavioral inhibition (BI). It has been studied extensively by the Harvard developmental psychologist Jerome Kagan and his colleagues.

When faced with unfamiliar situations or people or with unexpected changes, children with high BI have emotional outbursts or become fearful and inhibited. Toddlers identified with high BI sometimes retain these characteristics into adolescence, becoming teens who do not do well with change or unexpected events.

There is also evidence that the way we are wired interacts with the way we are raised. Nathan Fox, professor of human development at the University of Maryland, and his colleagues pointed out in their review of parenting practices that a limit-setting parenting style actually tends to decrease BI in temperamental infants by the time they are three. This should be of particular interest to the parents of children who display dramatic, negative reactions to new or unexpected events, as many such parents wonder whether taking more control will somehow stifle their children's development.

Our most compelling scientific evidence for why children who are sensitive to road map changes explode might be found in a group of children followed by Kagan and his colleagues in their long-term study of child temperament. Rates of phobic disorder — those highly emotional reactions to unexpected events or surprises — were significantly higher in inhibited children than in uninhibited children. Rates of oppositional behavior were significantly higher in uninhibited children than in inhibited children. In sum, explosive children tend to have a whole different personality type than oppositional defiant children, with tension as the main component.

Understanding such differences between explosive children and oppositional children is profoundly important. The current tendency to put labels such as "oppositional" or "defiant" on tense, rigid, or easily frustrated children who blow up when faced with unexpected events or requests from their parents or teachers is entirely wrong. The evidence points instead to the possibility that such children overreact, withdraw, or dig in their heels because the lower structures of their brains respond automatically to unexpected events by sending intense danger signals to the higher parts of their brains, not because they are trying to challenge authority.

That intense brain response takes much longer to describe than to actually occur. Let's return to Tyler 2, the boy who could not deal with his mother making an unexpected stop at a store. When a rigid, highly reactive child's road map fails to pan out as expected, the sensory cortex of the brain immediately increases alertness, and the child begins to feel very, very anxious. *Tyler 2's mom makes a sudden turn into a parking lot, telling everyone in the car that she just remembered she needs to stop at the nursery for some plant food.* A change in plans is frightening to explosion-prone children because of their belief that they know what is going to happen next. *Tyler 2's mind begins to race. This wasn't in the plan; we were headed to Target!* Their respiration becomes shallow and rapid. Their heart rate increases, along with their blood pressure and muscle tone. The amygdala begins to fire signals up to the prefrontal area of the brain. Panic! *"Mom, what are we doing here? Mom!"* Coagulants are dumped into the bloodstream, one of Mother Nature's protective mechanisms to decrease bleeding in case we get cut during a life-and-death struggle. The adrenal glands begin to pump epinephrine as the sympathetic nervous system powers up. *"Mom! Goddammit, Mom, what are we doing here?"* When the fight-or-flight mechanism swings into full operational mode, all hell breaks loose. *"MOM!"*

Even the tiniest child in the midst of a meltdown becomes remarkably strong and almost impossibly hard to restrain once he or she starts to kick and flail. These children scream as if their lives depended on it if you try to hold them still to calm them down, to keep them from hitting you or others, or to prevent them from destroying your home. Their bodies and brains are so pumped up with chemicals and hormones that they are locked and loaded and ready to rock and roll.

It would be entirely appropriate to rock and roll, to fight or flee, should they really be undergoing a life-threatening attack.

Consider it: this is one of nature's prime methods of helping to ensure the survival of the species. Thirty thousand years ago, when humans were roaming the savanna, if their brains remained calm and placid instead of clicking into emergency mode when they turned a corner and came upon a saber-toothed tiger, they might have been tempted to try to pet the thing. That would not have boded well for the production of offspring and the survival of their particular branch of the ancestral tree. But clicking into emotional overdrive just because your friend is not waiting for you at school or because your mom stops unexpectedly to get plant food is not appropriate and does not make sense to most observers. Yet this is how children with road map issues act. Their behavior changes from normal one moment to high drama or fight mode the next, as if someone had flipped a switch.

With all of this in mind, allow me to suggest that we abandon negative descriptors such as "oppositional" and "defiant" when referring to tense, behaviorally inhibited children who explode. Such terms do not paint a truthful picture of what these children are going through and do not point us in the right direction for how to treat them. Although it's unlikely that we will really abandon such terms because they are so descriptive of a child's observable behavior, we should, at the very least, use them with a great deal more care and thought. We are, after all, talking about children.

Transition Tantrums

By now you understand that road map meltdowns are strong emotional responses to virtually any event or change that a child does not anticipate, such as his favorite cartoon getting canceled on Saturday morning or being served strawberry ice cream when he expected chocolate. But we need to bore just a bit farther down into explosions to be more precise about their other causes. Specifically, we also need to talk about transitions.

If you are the parent of a child who explodes, you probably already know that transition times can be especially difficult for him. Let's look at two types of transitions that cause children to explode: simple transitions and ABX transitions.

The term "simple transitions" does not imply that they are easy for a child to make. Instead, it refers to a particular type of transition. Children's lives, like those of adults, are filled with two-step events in which they have to stop doing activity A and start doing activity B. These are simple transitions. Some children make these transitions easily; others do not. For them, it goes something like this: You say, "Please turn off your video game and come to dinner." Your child's response: Ignition! Blastoff!

Like all children, once an explosion-prone child has settled into an activity and is happy with what he is doing, he is loath to give it up. Pay particular attention to this notion of "give it up." For certain children, a request that they make a simple transition is tantamount to a demand that they give up the one thing that could possibly keep them happy. This is why they respond to your request the way you or I might respond to a demand to stop what we are doing and go jump into a dark hole, without a clue as to what is at the bottom, or even if there is a bottom.

An ABX transition occurs when, for example, your child is with you in the car and anticipates that you will be going from point A to point B (say, from the hardware store to the drugstore), but you stop at point X (say, the nursery). Or it could occur at the mall, when your child thinks you are leaving store A and headed to store B, only to have you detour to store X. Most children adapt to such an unexpected stop reasonably well, possibly only grumbling, "Why do we have to stop here?" Others do not react well at all.

One boy I worked with was so sensitive to ABX transitions that he had to have the itinerary in writing before he could comfortably go with his mother on her Saturday errands. His mother (who was single and had no one to leave him with) hated this, because it meant that she had to take the time to organize in her own mind exactly where they would go first, second, third, and so on. Trips with him always degenerated into an argument. "Mom, you *promised* we would go to Wal-Mart first, then Dillard's, and then Revco. You didn't say we would go to the dry cleaner before we went to Revco. You said we would go *after* Revco!" This boy would get so worked up that he would be unable to accept any of the standard answers, such as "It was more convenient to do it this way." He would scream, "But you *promised*!" and begin to kick the back of his mother's seat as she drove. At some point, as his frustration over being faced with a situation in which his road map and reality were no longer a match increased, he would begin to rant and rave. "You lied to me, Mom! You're a liar!"

Restoring the Peace in Three Steps

You can use a three-step process to deal with road map meltdowns and transition tantrums if it becomes clear that these are the underlying causes of your child's explosive behavior. When used appropriately, the techniques we are about to discuss can have a remarkably rapid, positive impact on your child. They are easy to follow because they are based on common sense.

The first step is clarification. You must ask yourself what you believe adults should do when faced with an out-of-control child. The second step involves learning a set of techniques that will get your child to think about his or her own behavior and its effect on others, something exceedingly important for children who explode again and again. The third step involves using these techniques to teach your child to get through situations that typically cause explosions.

It's hugely important to keep age at the forefront of your thinking about road map meltdowns and transition tantrums. The reason for this is that you cannot talk to a three- or four-year-old child the same way that you can talk to a four-and-a-half- or five-year-old child. You will have to adjust your strategies and expectations accordingly.

Step One: Clarifying Your Parenting Philosophy

As a parent, you have the right to know my viewpoint prior to adopting any of my methods. My philosophy is that it is the parent's obligation to teach his or her child how to act, regardless of how that child might wish to act at any given moment. This does not mean that I want to remove free will or diminish a child's spirit—I love happy, inventive, independent children and do my best to train parents and children in this viewpoint. However, being happy, inventive, and independent does not preclude acting in a polite manner when things don't go your way.

Anyone who loves children and who has raised children knows intuitively that a young mind can be a faulty device when it comes to deciding how to act. Saying this is not being disrespectful of children. It is simply stating a fact central to their need for adult guidance and feedback. We know from studying development, for example, that as children age, they are more able to do what is referred to as "probabilistic thinking." What this means in real-world terms—no big surprise to anyone who has raised a child—is that the older you get, the better you are at anticipating the outcome of your own behavior.

I ask parents to consider several points as they go about clarifying how they wish to respond to their child's explosions.

- Never assume that a child is simply a brat because he appears to explode for no reason at all. Such a viewpoint relegates that child to the position of damaged human being, an intolerable viewpoint when looking at any child. Remember, no child explodes over nothing, and no child explodes over everything. There are certain situations and events that set him off. Determining what sets a child off will almost always tell you what treatment strategy to use.
- Never assume that you know why your child blew sky-high. You have to talk to her, watch her, and think deeply about

patterns in her behavior to find hints about what sets her off. Granted, it will be difficult for a child under the age of four to give you any useful information, and children up to the age of six can typically provide only fragments of a situation, biased toward their own viewpoints. However, listening is the only way to truly read your child's mind.

- It is absolutely imperative that you do your best not to respond emotionally to your child's meltdowns by becoming highly emotional yourself. Yelling and screaming at a child who is in the midst of a meltdown is like trying to put out a fire by dousing it with gasoline and will make your child feel frantically unsafe. Wait until you are calm to discuss the fact that his behavior was not acceptable.
- You are under no obligation to stand by and watch your child go on a rampage of flipping furniture, stomping on toys, or hitting others. Doing nothing is, in fact, likely to reinforce violent behavior and make it more frequent, not less. Use the least amount of influence or power required to interrupt an episode of explosive behavior. If talking works, use it. Likewise, if moving the child to another area works, use it. However, if you come to a point where there is no other way to prevent the child from harming himself or herself or others or no other way to prevent her from destroying the house, you may certainly use gentle restraint. More on this later in this chapter.

Step Two: Implementing the Big Kid Program

The second step involves learning techniques designed to get your child to think about his behavior and to think about what he should do instead of blowing a gasket when faced with an unexpected event.

Let's talk about kids in the three- to six-year-old age range first. If we are smart, we will learn to see the world through their eyes.

From about three years of age and up, a child's most powerful fantasies revolve around being "big" and not being thought of by others as "little." I like to know how kids actually view themselves, so I always ask the youngest children I see at my office, "Are you a big kid or a little kid?" The few children who tell you that they are "little" are often describing their physical size. They usually think of themselves as "big," even though they are physically small. Granted, there are some kids who think of themselves as "little." I often find that these children have a harder time controlling themselves than kids who think of themselves as "big," and one of the early steps in working with them is to get them to aspire to be "big."

One example of a tiny child who thought of herself as big and potent was an angelic three-and-a-half-year-old girl whose mother described her as a "tantrum machine." I asked if she was a big girl or a little girl. She stood by my desk in her tiny tennis shoes, leg warmers, corduroy skirt, and sweater, with bows in her hair. She held her arms out to her sides, palms up, and looked herself over. She finally looked back up at me with a puzzled expression, as if I were the biggest idiot on the planet. "I'm big!" she said.

Several days later, I asked the same question to a boy who was just slightly older. He also stood still and posed for me, drawing himself up to his full height. While his language skills were not equal to those of the girl, as is frequently the case for boys early in their development, his response was nonetheless interesting. He said, "My head way up high," indicating that he believed himself to be a force to be reckoned with. I replied, "Dude, you are so tall that your feet go all the way to the floor," to which he smiled proudly.

I ask parents to take advantage of the way children think by splitting a young child's world into two dimensions when giving feedback on behavior: big versus little. In truth, many parents are already using such feedback when they say things like "I want you to act like a big kid." When using the big kid program, parents label everything that is good, everything worth having and doing, as "big." For example, age-appropriate behavior is described as "big guy" or "big girl" behavior: "I really like the way you're acting. You're being a big guy right now," or "Look how great you are acting. You're in the big girl zone!"

All treats become "big kid treats," and it goes without saying that the only way you can access the big stuff in life is by acting big. Popsicles are "big kid Popsicles," chips are "big kid chips," cookies are "only for big kids," and so on. The same extends to toys and other fun activities.

I am not immune to the fact that when we use the word "big," which obviously equals good, positive, and desirable, the word "little" is also in play and has a negative value. There are many ways this must be examined, because it is an important issue.

Young children naturally tend to think in dichotomies. Things are good or bad, big or small, tasty or yucky, with very little in between. Big versus little makes everything clear for them. Until they begin to mature, all the shades of gray between the extremes just get muddled in their minds.

Some parents object to the use of the word "little" and take the position that telling a child that she is acting "little" is a form of guilt training or guilt induction. I understand their concerns.

I once worked with an exuberantly joyful five-year-old girl who found delight in the world in a way that all of us could learn from. Her main issues were that she was squirmy to distraction at school and continued to have bathroom accidents. Her teacher was apparently harsh toward her, even though she was reading at the third-grade level and was a math whiz. Her father, who had been treated harshly as a child, explained to me with misty eyes that he needed to find the most positive methods possible to help his daughter overcome her issues, as he and her mother did not want her spirit dampened the way that his had been. She responded wonderfully and with great laughter to my telling her that our goal was to have her put the poopy in the potty like the big girls do, and that if she worked hard on it, we would make sure that there would be plenty of big girl rewards. Her parents reinforced her hard work and success with verbal praise, hugs, and big girl treats and privileges, and she did everything we asked her to do, with never a punishing word being spoken.

Any compassionate listener will understand the issues raised by the dad I just mentioned. But I've also met parents who have told me that they do not believe it is "right" or "fair" for them to judge their children's behavior in any way, shape, or form. I recall being dressed down by a mother who told me that she intended to let her son become who he would be without any interference from others. It made me wonder whether she believed that children just sort of unfold over time and that no one should do anything to hamper, impede, guide, or influence them. Her position reminded me of Frederick II, the early-thirteenth-century Holy Roman emperor, who wanted to see what language children would speak if allowed to develop on their own, without adult interference and without hearing any language from their adult caretakers. They never spoke a word, and apparently the lack of nurturing, interactive attention prevented all of them from making it out of childhood.

In the end, there are easy ways to temper concerns about words and the nature of parents' feedback. First, I instruct parents to keep the word "little" in reserve and to use it only when absolutely necessary. You will help a child modify her explosive behavior a lot faster by pumping her up for her successes than by pointing out her failures. Some of the younger kids I see get so goosed up by slapping hands with me and having me reward them with paper airplanes that will do loops and turns that they cannot wait to get home and do what is necessary to stay in the big kid zone.

If you have to use a term such as "little" when your child is acting in a clearly unacceptable manner and not paying attention to your urgings to get back into the big kid zone, keep in mind that it is not in the least comparable to telling a child that he is a bad human being. It is simply giving the child feedback on his behavior in terms that are not muddled or made too vague out of a misplaced desire to explain adult judgments to little kids. When done properly—which means calmly and lovingly, with gentle humor attached and always with the promise of a positive outcome—it makes kids hopeful about improving: "Uh-oh, I'm seeing too much little kid behavior from you right now. I want you to get yourself back in the big kid zone pronto, please, so you can keep on having fun and using your big kid stuff!"

THE BRAIN GAME

There is a second part to the big kid program—the concept of the big kid brain and the little kid brain. Children also accept this concept readily.

It is important to hear from parents who have used the techniques that I describe in this section. A mother whose son was four and prone to massive tantrums that interrupted every trip to the grocery store or every attempt to go out to dinner had this to say about using the terms "big guy" and "little guy" with her son:

> This is the "miracle" code for him, and for us. It is a positive term that helps him get back on track. It's in his own language. He completely understands big guy/little guy. And he strives to be big guy. Plus, using big guy/little guy calms us—there is no shaming or blaming involved. It's very simple—it's a clear term for all of us. He knows exactly what behaviors to change and what we're asking of him.

Here is what another mother wrote when asked to assess this type of treatment. Her child came to my office for only five sessions. Much of that time was spent training the mother in the techniques discussed in this book.

P. was six years old and in first grade. He and I were butting heads all the time. I felt like he was not listening to me the first time I asked for something to be done. I too was at fault because I would lose my temper. I did not like the road we were on. Quite frankly I did not feel good about myself and how P. and I were interacting.

The big kid/little kid phrase worked wonders! Since I have two small boys, I brought them both in to stay on the same track. I used it right away, and the boys' behavior changed instantly. I last met with you six months ago, and the big/little phrase still works. All I have to do is ask them to use their big brain and their behavior changes. Of all the suggestions that you gave me to help steer the boys, the big boy brain has really worked.

I tell kids, as well as parents, that anyone who comes to my office better have a sense of humor, because there will be some teasing and some fun in the midst of dealing with serious issues. For example, kids get a kick out of it when I tell them about the medieval notion of the homunculus, a tiny person inside each of us who controls what we do. I use that idea to tell them that everybody has a big kid brain and a little kid brain, and that when they listen to what the big kid brain is telling them to do, they will hardly ever get into trouble. I also point out that the little kid brain is always trying to get control, to become the "boss brain." I tell them that the problem is that whenever the little kid brain becomes the boss brain, it always gets them in trouble. Some children in the high four-year-old range understand all of this, and most five-year-olds understand it easily.

While this might sound like silly fun and games, it is actually a central part of the treatment. Using terms such as "big" and "little" serves as the external feedback part of the treatment model. External feedback is useless unless a child actually begins to think about his behavior. Otherwise, the child won't care about your judgments.

This is where the brain game comes in. It forms the groundwork for a cognitive therapy technique, the internal thinking part of treatment. I ask parents to play it frequently with children who explode, because it can help them to resist the thoughts and feelings that invariably get them in trouble when they are angry. Children who react violently or aggressively have been found to have mental "scripts" that unfortunately guide them step by step to a bad outcome when a situation displeases them. We must do everything possible to teach them to change the way they think so that they can respond more appropriately. Their age demands, however, that the techniques be simple.

When I play the brain game with children, I tell them that I am going to pretend that I am part of their brain. I tell them that I am going to be the little kid part of their brain and they are going to be the big kid part. I point out that they cannot afford to let the little kid brain be the boss brain because it will always get them in trouble. It will be much better for them to make sure that the big kid brain continues to be the boss brain.

Then I tell them that we are going to have a brain argument. As the little kid brain, I am going to try to get to be the boss brain. They will be the big kid brain, and their job is to argue with me and not let the little kid brain get to be the boss brain. Following is the type of dialogue that I engage a child in when playing the brain game.

ME: Hey, our mom just told us to turn off the video game and come to dinner. We don't want to! Let's throw a fit!

CHILD: No, if we throw a fit, we'll get in trouble.

ME: We don't care. Let's go kick something!

CHILD: No! We're going to act big.

ME: I don't want to act big! I want us to have a great big fit right now!

CHILD: No! We're going to do what Mom told us to do.

ME: Let's tell her she's a bad mom for making us stop playing.

CHILD: No, if we do that, we'll get in trouble. I don't want to do that.

ME: Yes, we do want to do that.
CHILD: No! Let's act big!
ME: OK, OK, OK, you win! We'll act big!

Once I see that the child has gotten the point and is actually using clear logic, I let her know that she has made a good decision by deciding to act big. Then I give the child a high-five and watch her beam with pride over having been so smart as to keep out of trouble.

I encourage parents to play the brain game with their exploding children at any opportunity: while driving in the car, sitting around the house, taking a walk, and so on. Do it for only about a minute at a time, and end with praising the child for letting the big kid brain be the boss brain. It may take some coaching to get your child into the flow of the brain argument, as he may not know what to say at first. This is to be expected. Just give your child hints about what to say and make sure he has fun.

Why should you use a technique like the brain game? While you may be tempted to try to have a regular conversation with your young child about how to use internal self-talk and thoughts to control behavior, it is just not likely to go very far. With younger kids, you have to hook them by using simplicity and fun. Additionally, when you play the brain game with your child often, it gives you a chance to hear how he or she actually thinks. You can then offer feedback, corrections, or praise for your child's attempts at self-control.

Over the years, I have had many children tell me that they use the brain game to keep themselves out of trouble at home or at school. Also, it is not uncommon for children to ask me to play the brain game with them, because two things are guaranteed to happen when we do: (1) they have fun because I am animated and silly and I use a weird voice when I do it; and (2) they get to show off the part of their thinking that is the biggest and best part of themselves.

The mother of a five-year-old boy had this to say about the brain game:

> Once we started, it was fun and a great way to ease the anger and tension we were feeling in the beginning throes of a "little guy" episode. He really likes it, and it helps him to see what he's doing and gives him the control to change. It helps him to get a sense of what he wants to do rather than just reacting.

Another mother of a five-year-old boy, who was close to being removed from his private kindergarten, wrote:

> The brain game was one of his favorite games to play. It was easy to understand for me and him. It also gave him the feeling that he was just having fun, but he was actually learning.

My patient Patrick, who was five, put an interesting spin on the brain game for me. He told me that at school, his friend Ronnie told him to hold his finger on the water fountain and then press the button. When he did, Ronnie got sprayed in the face, and Patrick got in trouble for it. I asked Patrick if this was one of those times that his little guy brain had gotten to be his boss brain. He said no, what had happened was that he had let Ronnie be his boss brain, and this is why he got in trouble. This led us into an enjoyable round of role-playing, in which I pretended to be another kid trying to be his boss brain.

ME: Let's go tell that guy he smells like a skunk!
PATRICK: No, I don't want to act like that!
ME: Come on, it will be fun. He won't do anything.
PATRICK: It will make him sad. I don't like that.
ME: It won't make him sad. He'll think it's funny.
PATRICK: I told you no, I'm not going to do it.
ME: OK, OK, OK, you win.

Kids also like to hear that adults struggle with their own internal urges, because it normalizes their struggles. If they think they are the only ones struggling to control themselves, they begin to judge themselves negatively. Knowing that other people struggle, even adults, leaves them feeling much more positive and optimistic about the prospect of the big kid brain winning. For example, I tell them that when I drive home from work each night, I have to go past a Wendy's. When my little kid brain sees the Wendy's sign, it always says, "Frosty! I want a Frosssssssssss-teeeeeeeeee!"

Then I tell them that I have to do a brain argument with myself. My big kid brain says things such as "You haven't had dinner yet. It's not healthy to have dessert first," or "You don't need one of those every night, because you have to watch your weight. You can only have one every now and then."

BEYOND PRESCHOOL: WORKING WITH KIDS AGES EIGHT TO TEN

You have to be careful about the descriptive terms you use when you are talking to a child who is in the third grade and up. Many kids who are eight or older may still respond well to the term "big kid," but some will not. Some kids in the third grade and most kids in the fourth grade will turn up their noses at the notion of being described by adults as a "big kid," as it will strike them as too babyish. If you talk down to kids in this age range, you've lost them. But if you talk up to them by offering them alternative ways to act and clear, positive consequences for doing so, you may find them to be very cooperative and excited about solving their behavioral problems.

Follow this ground rule: If your child responds well to descriptors such as "big kid" and "big kid zone," feel free to use them. Once the term "big" has lost its potency, however, as it eventually will, use other words to talk about behavior: "I really liked the way you acted today. You did a great job." Or, "Things didn't go too well today. I'd like to see you act differently." Provide the specifics, without running on too long or lecturing.

With the nine- or ten-year-olds in particular, it is best to talk very straightforwardly about meltdowns and tantrums. The tenor of the discussion should be that the child displays these behaviors too often and it is your job as an adult to help him figure out why he explodes and to help him learn how not to. You should always give the child the benefit of the doubt by letting him know that you realize that he doesn't like to act that way and feels bad about it. You also should let him know that everyone makes such mistakes, including you. Tell your child that he should never waste a mistake by not learning from it.

I tell kids who come to my office that we don't talk about punishment as long as we know that a child is taking the change process seriously. Instead, we talk about rewards, and I guarantee that they will like the rewards for working hard to master their explosions. This typically delights them, because kids in the nine- and ten-year-old range almost always think that they are being brought to the psychologist's office to be punished or because someone thinks they are bad. While they may come to the first meeting in an apprehensive or resistant manner, they often leave happy. I believe that it is best to appeal to the part of an explosive child that wants to do better, rather than to rub her nose in the fact that she explodes.

Step Three: Using Exposure Therapy to Prevent Road Map Meltdowns

For many children, simply using terms such as "big kid" or telling them to use the brain game when you see them getting upset or explosive when faced with unexpected events or transitions will have a major impact on the way they act. If simple interventions like these result in a marked improvement, your job is mostly finished. But for some children, the explosions will persist. This leads us to the third part of helping children who explode due to road map and transition issues: teaching them to get through situations that typically make them melt down by actually exposing them to these situations.

First, a few words about exposure therapy. This is the notion that a person can overcome what frightens or bothers him or her through gradual, controlled exposure to it. This is a well-established treatment technique. Joseph Wolpe, the South African–born psychiatrist whose name is typically associated with the early theory of exposure therapy, referred to as desensitization, published his landmark book about the technique in 1958. A literature search on desensitization will turn up hundreds, if not thousands, of articles about it.

There is no consensus as to why exposure therapy works, but Professor Rudi De Raedt at Ghent University reports intriguing evidence that at some point during repeated exposure to whatever you fear, your brain begins to suppress the signals moving between the amygdala—that tiny ball of neurons that is the seat of strong emotions and fear responses—and the prefrontal cortex, the area of the brain associated with thinking and decision making. This change results in increased emotional control. This remarkable finding can help us move past vague talk therapies and medication-related treatment models to an understanding of how exposure therapy might alter the brain functioning of explosive children in a way that will give them permanent relief.

AN EXAMPLE OF REPEATED EXPOSURE

I worked with a nine-year-old boy named Adam who was always blowing up and trying to control everything. Adam was a tall, gangly kid who was reluctant to make eye contact. His mother described him as touchy and said that he did not have many friends. He tended to stay to himself and loved his video games. I got him to talk by showing him how to build those complicated paper airplanes I mentioned earlier, and we would toss them around while we talked. He was prone to road map meltdowns and transition tantrums and was particularly sensitive to ABX transitions. For example, if he was in the car with his mother and he thought that they were headed to Sam's Club but she stopped at Walgreens on the way, he would come unglued. He would yell, scream, demand to know why they had stopped, and remain upset, unpleasant, tearful, and prone to more dramatic outbursts for the rest of the day. He might calm down briefly if she bought him a treat, but that was no guarantee. Sometimes he would throw the treat down and continue to whimper bitterly.

His mother told me privately that she was on the verge of a nervous breakdown because of the stress of dealing with his explosions. She said that she walked on eggshells with him all day long and feared having anything happen that he did not expect because he would explode. She also feared for the type of man he would become if he did not change these behaviors. His brother, who was almost six years younger than Adam, would say to him, "I bigger than you."

My plan for treating Adam entailed exposing him frequently to the very situations that he did not like – unexpected changes in plans, unexpected stops at stores while driving with his mother, changes in what he was going to have for dinner, having to stop doing one activity and change to something else, and so on. I knew that at some point, his brain would get used to unexpected events if he had to deal with them frequently, just as I knew that his life would be full of tension and misery if he never overcame his aversion to the unexpected.

His mother was concerned about putting him through frequent exposure to unexpected events. Her question to me may mirror your own concern: "Should we put our children in situations that they obviously don't like?"

You cannot be a passive parent if you have an anxious, controlling, explosive child like Adam. It was guaranteed that he would be defensive about his behavior and would make every effort to avoid dealing with it. It was also guaranteed that he would be unlikely to remember his childhood in happy terms if he remained as he was. Sometimes helping a child learn more appropriate ways of responding to the world entails having him go through events that he would rather avoid but that he would be much better off mastering. Here are the assumptions about exposure therapy that I hope to get you to accept.

- Sheltering children from an event that causes meltdowns virtually guarantees that they will blow up every time they encounter it or a similar situation.
- Avoiding the situation will never allow children to work through what sets them off in the first place.
- Avoiding the situation tricks children into believing that they will never have to deal with it.
- Rapidly removing a child from the situation following a blowup, such as taking her home once she ignites over the possibility of going to a store she did not anticipate going to, leaves her with the illusion that blowing up is an escape hatch she can use to avoid situations she doesn't like. This will eventually increase the frequency of blowups instead of decreasing them. It is much better for children to master such unexpected events by becoming desensitized to them.
- By being overly protective of explosive children, you run the risk of turning them into emotional cripples.

Another reason that I asked Adam's parents to consider putting him through exposure therapy, which was guaranteed to make him uncomfortable at first, was to help him feel victorious about his life. Tense, brittle children do not like the way they act and wish desperately to be able to act differently, even though they will argue vigorously that it is the world that should change, not them. Another nine-year-old boy I know is a prime example of this. He blew up publicly and in a very embarrassing way when one of his classmates poked him and said, "I can draw better than you, nah nah na nah nah!" After his blowup, he felt so ashamed of himself that he retreated to a far corner of the playground, where he could be heard shouting to himself, "Why are you even alive? You don't deserve to be here!" Children like this child and Adam need a victory over their anxieties, worries, and fears. It will not be easily or cheaply won, but it is our obligation to devise methods that will help them overcome their fears.

There are several ways to use exposure therapy with explosive children. The easiest and most informal method involves sitting down with your child and telling him that you know that certain situations make him feel really cranky, angry, and explosive. Then explain that the fastest way to help him solve having blowups is to have him practice getting through these situations. Explain that this will mean gradually increasing the number of unexpected events and transitions in his life, and that you will give him feedback along the way about how he is handling himself.

For younger kids, be sure to use the brain game and feedback on being a big kid as you help your child work through this increase in unexpected events. Make sure that you tell both younger and older children that you understand that this will be hard work. Tell them that you will reward their hard work well, because you want them to see that they can master their lives and make these changes. In general, once your child is no longer exploding in response to the unexpected events or transitions that formerly plagued him, your work is complete. Remember, however, that childhood is messy and kids will never gain complete control of all their emotions in every situation. The goal is simply to help your child handle unexpected events and transitions the way most kids in the same age group do.

With kids who are exceptionally explosive, like Adam, I sometimes use a more formalized approach. (My preference is to use the informal approach first.) Let me review: I asked Adam's parents to sit down with him at home for a meeting. I should add that parents will obviously have to adjust the content and length of the meeting to suit their child's age. There are some common points, however, that differ very little with age. For example, the best time to call such a meeting is on a weekend during a period of peace. It is never a good idea to try to have a serious talk with your child about his behavior just after he has exploded. Also, you don't want this meeting to conflict with homework.

I suggested to Adam's parents that they have something to snack on or drink during this meeting to set a friendly tone and to help avoid having him become defensive. Their job was to tell him in a friendly manner that they realized he had more trouble with unexpected events and transitions than he would like and to offer examples if necessary. They also were to tell him that as his parents, it was their job to come up with ways to help him deal with those situations better.

I cautioned them to remain *parental,* which is my term for being nondefensive and open to listening to what he had to say, while also conveying that it was their responsibility as the parents to do whatever was necessary to help him solve the problem of exploding. I told them that it was fine if he did not agree with them or said that he did not want to change. They would in turn explain that if they saw him working hard on the program, there would be plenty of rewards and fun. If they judged him not to be working hard, it would mean that the work would simply take a lot longer. I told them to be exceptionally firm that not working on solving his explosions was not an option.

SIMULATIONS

This is the part where the parents use their own talent for drama. Simulations work well with kids between five and eight, although they worked well with Adam, who was nine, as well. Ideally, you should do this on the same night that you sit down and talk with your child about the program. The purpose of doing simulations is, first of all, to get the child to lighten up and not be so worried about the process. Explain that it will actually be fun as well as instructive. It is also important to make your child aware that she is not the only one who struggles with such situations. Don't be surprised if she thinks this way—many kids do. Thinking that she is the only kid who displays such behaviors will make her believe that she is somehow damaged, which in turn will make her less likely to think about it or talk about it at all.

With this in mind, do a role play in front of your child in which one parent plays a child and the other parent plays a parent. You can role-play any sort of road map or transition issue. For example, role-play a simple transition, one in which you have the "parent" ask the "child" to make an unexpected transition such as having to stop watching TV and come to dinner, or stop playing a video game and start doing homework. In this scenario, have the "child" do a total meltdown—flopping around, screaming, crying, stomping, huffing and puffing, and so on. It is critically important that you do this with humor and that you make your child laugh in the process.

One important ground rule to follow in these simulations is to not pretend to be your own child—pretend to be some other child who has trouble with transitions. While it might be instructive in some ways for your child to see how he acts, this has to be balanced against the risk of his thinking you are making fun of him.

After you do the role play demonstrating the meltdown, explain to your child that you are now going to redo the role play, this time demonstrating how you want him to act and think in the future. Replay the same scenarios you used previously, but this time demonstrate how the "child" gets through the transitions successfully. Have the "child" use a number of tools to get through the scenario. If your real child is between five and seven years of age, have the "child" play the brain game with the "parent." Let the "parent" be the little kid brain and the "child" be the big kid brain.

LITTLE KID BRAIN: Hey, Mom said stop playing the video game and go get all of our dirty laundry together. We hate this. Let's blow up bigtime!

BIG KID BRAIN: No way. This is just a surprise. It's no big deal.

LITTLE KID BRAIN: We hate surprises! Let's kick something!
BIG KID BRAIN: No way! Surprises are no big deal. We can get through surprises without blowing up.
LITTLE KID BRAIN: No we can't! They're too hard!
BIG KID BRAIN: No they are not. We can do it without exploding!
LITTLE KID BRAIN: OK, you win.

After you go through this, it will be time for your real child to be the simulator who melts down, and following that the simulator who gets through the situations smoothly. Your child may initially be confused about what he is supposed to say during the role play. Be prepared to coach him through this, something you can easily do by whispering to him what he should say. The main point is to help the child arrive at the idea that he can use his own thoughts to resist the urge to explode. You are likely to be surprised by how quickly most kids catch on.

While some children will think that the role play is hilarious and will have fun doing it, others will not like the idea at all. They will argue that they have learned enough from watching you to be able to cope with unexpected situations. I can appreciate their apprehension and shyness about the task, but you must point out that it is unlikely that they could learn how to play an instrument just by going to a concert or learn how to hit a baseball just by watching a baseball game on TV. Explain that the only way to learn any new skill is to practice it. Be gently insistent about this, because there is little chance that when push comes to shove, your child will be able to use the skills you have demonstrated unless she has practiced them.

Are there times when you should skip the simulation phase altogether and use just talk instead? Yes, but probably not with children age six or under. Some older children will find doing simulations too "lame" or "boring." With these children, having them sit quietly and imagining themselves getting through unexpected transitions and events smoothly might serve the needs of this stage of treatment. This visualizing, known as *competence imagery,* has been shown to be effective in managing anxiety. It can also be a useful technique in situations where children overreact to unexpected events or transitions.

It goes without saying that any technique will do little good if your child does not take it seriously. If you can see that nothing good is going to come out of trying to force your child to use simulation or imagery, do not use either. Shift your strategy to simply discussing the techniques with your child in order to explain that the focus will now be on helping him or her to get through unexpected events smoothly.

There is a final caveat about simulations: if your child is between the ages of three and four and a half, the simulations and imaging procedures described here will be too advanced. While it certainly will not hurt to try the role plays and demonstrations with kids who have reached four and a half, some parents will find that their kids just don't get it because they are not mature enough to understand all the implications of the procedure. Given this, I typically tell parents of children less than four and a half not to bother with simulations or other techniques, and to consider simply upping the number of unexpected events and transitions in their lives in order to desensitize them to the unexpected.

The main point to remember is that for your young child to learn to deal with unexpected events appropriately, he or she must be exposed to them on a consistent basis. A useful analogy to consider is that of babies who have been exposed to normal levels of household noise from a young age compared to those who have been sheltered from every possible noise by well-meaning but misguided parents. Babies with no noise exposure will wake up at the drop of a pin and have difficulty settling down unless the house is as quiet as Tut's tomb. Babies exposed to regular noise will sleep more soundly.

WEEK ONE OF EXPOSURE THERAPY: PRACTICING WITH REAL TRANSITIONS AND UNEXPECTED EVENTS

Ideally, this step should begin the day after you do the practice simulations with your child. Tell your child that in this first week, you will begin to have him or her practice successfully getting through many transitions and surprises every day. Tell the child that you will give her a five-minute warning prior to any transition, although you will refuse to tell her what the transition specifically is going to be before it happens. In reality, if you find that five minutes is too long, you can shorten the time between the warning and the transition to whatever period works best for your child. Tell the child that while the transitions might seem somewhat artificial, you will still expect a good effort.

During this week, you should try to have your child go through at least one unexpected transition per hour. Remain flexible, because there is no reason to treat this like some "five-step" program carved in stone. Adjust the frequency of the transitions to a level that your child can both tolerate and learn from. Try not to skip too many opportunities, as this will prevent your child from learning to deal with transitions peacefully.

Use simple, real-world transitions, such as turning off a video game to do homework, turning off the TV to take some clean laundry up to her room, or stopping playing with blocks or Legos to take out the trash. Deliver lots of verbal praise when you see your child trying hard to get through these transitions smoothly.

You may also need to use ABX transitions, such as alerting your child while you are driving that in a few minutes you will make an unexpected stop. Do not tell the child where you are going to stop, just tell her that she has to get through it smoothly. Such a technique gives you a chance to teach your child that not all ABX transitions are bad. Your unexpected stop may be at an ice cream parlor to get a milk shake or at her favorite store to get a reward for her hard work. Also remember to throw in lots of unexpected changes and surprises – give your child unexpected items in his lunch, take a different route to school, move his furniture around, and so on.

An important aspect of this is to debrief your child after each transition or surprise. If your child gets through these well, ask what she thought or did that made it go easily. Do not readily accept "I don't know" as an answer. If your child truly does not know – and often the younger kids will not be able to articulate a reason – do your best to help her figure out what worked.

If your child did not get through the transitions and surprises well, debriefing will provide the opportunity to discuss what was hard about it and how she could have handled it better. Your job here is to remain hopeful that the child will get through the next transition or unexpected change better. Do your best to avoid punishments and negative consequences if your child melts down. I much prefer insight to punishment.

If your child continues to explode during week one, you may have to go back to doing simulations. It is possible that the pace has been too quick or the child needs more time to learn the coping skills by doing more simulations. Also, it is likely that some children will continue to melt down and explode in an attempt to get you to give up on the whole transition and unexpected event thing. Do not cave in! Remember, children who explode at the drop of a hat are not likely to change their response style without considerable effort on your part and on theirs.

In actuality, "week one" can run for as many days or weeks as is necessary. The more transitions and unexpected events your child is exposed to, the more desensitized he or she will become to them, leading to a decrease in the number of explosive episodes. It is very important to communicate to your child that you do not intend to give up, because it is critical that the child learn how to deal with unexpected events without melting down. It is equally important that you resolve not to go back to walking on eggshells with your child.

WEEK TWO OF EXPOSURE THERAPY: REALITY COMES CALLING

This phase begins after—and only after—your child has been generally successful with the week one transitions. Success means that you see your child making a definite attempt to use the skills you have covered when faced with transitions and unexpected events, and that the frequency of explosions is rapidly declining. In week two, you sit down with your child again and explain that the unexpected events and transitions will continue to occur at a high frequency, but now there will be no warnings. Reiterate your commitment to providing big rewards for effort. If your child is doing well after several days, begin to experiment with frequency, such as having more transitions one day than another so that your child does not find the program to be too predictable.

During week two, be sure to also continue to expose your child to frequent unexpected situations that have nothing to do with simple transitions and ABX transitions in order to help him realize that just because he expects something to happen, that does not mean it will. You will, of course, tell him that you intend to do this. Use techniques such as telling him in the morning to have a good day at school and saying that when he gets home, you will fix burgers for dinner. Serve spaghetti instead. Tell him that you are going to pick up some strawberry ice cream when you go to the store, but bring home peach instead. Rearrange the furniture in your den or living room. Change the route you use to take your child to school, to the mall, or to a friend's house. Tell him that you are going to one restaurant, then drive by it and say, "I changed my mind," and go to another. (This would be a good time to make this a positive surprise by ultimately going to a restaurant that you know he likes.) Go to the movie store alone, ostensibly to pick up a particular movie to watch. Tell the child that it was unavailable and that you had to get a different movie. Be inventive, presenting the child with transitions, situations, and surprises that you know he typically has difficulty with.

During this period, you may also find that it is necessary to work on meltdowns and explosions in settings other than your home or car. One nine-year-old girl I know pinches her mother and hisses muted insults at her in a store if her mother does not stop at an aisle that the girl expected to stop at, or if her mother goes into a store at the mall that the girl did not expect to go into. It is exceptionally important in her treatment to point out where all of these rugged transitions take place and to have her return to these places over and over to give her practice getting through the events successfully.

Many mothers tell me that it is virtually impossible to go into a grocery store (or any store, for that matter) without their children melting down. I use a particular procedure for this. Using the grocery store as an example, I suggest the following: Take your child to the grocery store. Put a few boxed items in the cart. Your intent is to move around the store but not do any real shopping. You are actually waiting for your child to have the explosion that he always has. Once the explosion occurs, take your child out to the car until he or she is calm. Reiterate that you expect him to act big in the store and that in a minute you will be going back into the store to finish your shopping. Do not, under any circumstances, take the child home. Go back into the store, find your cart, and continue moving around the store. I have had mothers set aside several hours for this procedure, taking the child back out to the car repeatedly if the child melts down, then back into the store. Remember, every young child has some store meltdowns, but this procedure can help your child get used to going shopping with you in a more peaceful manner.

If you find that exposing your child to unexpected events without any warning is just too much for him, you should return to using warnings for another week, then give the no warning phase another try. In general, when children fail during the no warning phase, it says that they need more of the highly programmed and supportive procedures used with warnings. The beauty of this particular program is its flexibility.

At some point, your child will break out of the explosive mode

One mother offered a lengthy review of how learning about road maps and transitions affected her eleven-year-old son's life.

> At home, B. was becoming very defiant, and his defiance would often end in outbursts I called preteenage temper tantrums. These tantrums included yelling, throwing things, slamming doors, and warning that no matter what we did, he would not obey or go along. B. was quite verbal and would not allow us to separate from him or ignore the outbursts. He would literally repeat a phrase over and over for ten or fifteen minutes and would follow us from room to room to get a reaction. By the beginning of school the tantrums were becoming more violent and they were occurring closer together. Their duration had also lengthened, lasting hours and sometimes into the next day.
>
> Initially, we had B. observed and tested for ADHD. The result was what I expected: he had ADHD tendencies but he was not a clear-cut case of ADD [attention deficit disorder] or ADHD. The decision of putting him on medication fell to us. B.'s pediatrician referred us to you [the author] as an intermediate or alternative step.
>
> At our first meeting with you, I described B.'s behavior. I told [you] that it seemed that the tantrums were always preceded by B. not getting his way or being told "no" to a request.
>
> Immediately when you explained that B.'s behavior sounded like difficulty with "road maps and transitions," B. and I both began to feel better. The description that you gave us of people getting a plan or a road map in their mind and then having great difficulty transitioning to a new plan, usually someone else's plan, fit B. exactly. I sat in your office replaying all the recent tantrum scenes in my mind, and I realized they all fit the description. B. and I felt instantly better just having this insight.
>
> I began to point out every time a situation fit into the "road map/transition" scenario. I used the word "transition"

to trigger B.'s realization of what was occurring. For example, I would say, "I can see this is a difficult transition for you." The first few times were minor events—he needed to take his shower before bedtime but wanted to watch the end of a TV program—and he grinned as he turned off the TV, recognizing what was happening. Since then, many more serious situations have arisen. These events have been difficult, but the results are dramatically better. My husband and I have been empowered to defuse a potentially explosive situation when it occurs. When we recognize that an outburst or tantrum is about to occur, we will remind B. that he must adapt to the transition at hand. Most importantly, B. has been empowered to understand his own tendencies and to better control them. Our home life has become more peaceful, and we have more fun together.

I would rate his original symptoms a nine out of ten. Not a ten because he never destroyed property or hurt someone during a tantrum. Today I would rate B.'s symptoms a three out of ten. He is doing very well. He is sometimes resistant to recognizing a transition but always, ultimately, responds in a positive way.

---

and will be able to deal with the world as it is. Your job at this point is to live up to your end of the bargain and substantially reward your child's hard work. You should also expect that when your child goes through periods of high stress or through a developmental shift (beginning a new grade in school, for example), he or she may return to the old patterns. Sometimes, for no apparent reason, a child will simply return to his old habits, prompting you to think that your efforts have failed. You have not failed. Children often regress. The main point is to talk with your child about returning quickly to handling unexpected transitions and events successfully.

The Sensitive Issue of Restraint

There is a reason that I have chosen to save the issue of restraining children who are out of control until the end of this chapter. It is because restraint should be the last technique that you turn to when working with a child who has road map and transition problems, and it should be used as infrequently as possible. By any standard, it will be better in the long run to spend your time helping your child learn self-control skills than to have to take control physically.

With that said, I encounter children every day who insistently attempt to clobber their parents, teachers, and peers and to wreck their homes and classrooms. Should you stand by and do nothing?

The parents of children who do not display explosive, aggressive behavior typically think that such behavior is due to poor parenting. One mother I am currently working with, a kindergarten teacher, tells me just what a humbling experience it has been to have changed her thinking from "No child of mine will ever act that way" to "How do I deal with this?" once she had children.

It is also common for the parents of explosive children to think that their child is the only child who is behaving in such a manner and to refuse to admit it to anyone. The reason for this, of course, is that they are embarrassed by it and afraid that they will be labeled as inadequate parents. It is this embarrassed silence that leads to the myth that such behavior among children is exceedingly rare. The research of others, as well as my own experience, tells me differently. We know, for example, that disruptive behavior, which includes aggression and noncompliance, is the most common reason that preschool children are seen for psychological treatment.

The issue of how to respond to an out-of-control child is admittedly complex. The mother of an explosive boy named Marco, who was almost four, brought a videotape to my office. The tape had been made by a teacher and showed Marco in the midst of a full-blown meltdown at his preschool. The teacher had actually given the tape to Marco's mother to prove to her how bad his behavior was at school because the mother said that he never acted out violently at home. What it really illustrated, however, was how muddled adults have become about dealing with children who are out of control.

By the time the teacher started filming Marco, he was already several minutes into his meltdown. This had apparently been induced by his not being allowed to have an extra fruit cup during snack time because his behavior earlier in the morning had been aggressive toward the other children. All of the other children had been removed from the room – standard operating procedure at many schools when a child becomes explosive and assaultive. Marco was flipping over chairs, sweeping objects off tabletops and desks with his arm, and trying to hit and kick the teacher as she tried to keep him at arm's length while also running the video camera.

He pulled down a stack of mats that were used at naptime and attempted to whack the teacher with one. He then turned his attention to a stack of cots about five feet high. In a way that illustrates perfectly just how much trouble kids have anticipating the consequences of their behavior, he gave the pile a jerk, bringing the cots down on top of him. Seconds later, Marco burst from beneath the tangle of cots like an enraged miniature King Kong and steamed toward the teacher, fists clenched and ready to take another bite out of her. The last thing I saw on the tape before it ran out was the teacher trying to reason with him in the midst of his barrage, saying things such as "Marco, *please* don't do that," "Marco, *please* calm down," and "Marco, *please* stop."

Marco's teacher was most definitely operating under school policies stating that a teacher cannot restrain or place hands on a child, even when he is out of control. Most schools have at least one individual, typically an assistant principal or security officer but also often a teacher, who is certified to use restraint when necessary. This person was obviously not present during Marco's explosion. What Marco learned from this situation was that he was large and in charge, that he could do virtually anything he wanted, and that no teacher could stop him, not even if she used the magic word "please" over and over.

We have all heard one too many stories about parents who, in the name of discipline, abuse their children or treat them so roughly that their spirits and self-concepts were damaged almost beyond repair. The sad legacy of these adults is that today the simple act of taking hold of a three-year-old who is in a full-tilt meltdown is seen as a violation of that child's integrity or an act of abuse. I cannot tell you exactly how many parents have told me that they are afraid they will be arrested if they take physical control of an out-of-control child and someone hears the child screaming in protest. I am positive that I have heard this worry expressed on hundreds of occasions.

There is no reason to equate restraining a thoroughly out-of-control child with physically abusing a child. I am sure that this opinion will outrage certain people, but this issue must be examined from several angles. First, it is important to stress that restraint as described in this book is not a form of punishment and should never be used for such a purpose. It should be used only as a behavior interruption technique in high-risk situations when nothing else will work, the same way you would physically restrain a child from jumping off of a second-story balcony or punching a window. It should be used only to keep a child from harming herself or others or from destroying her environment or belongings.

If you insist on using only talk and reason with a child who is out of control, your task may prove to be highly complicated. Often the individual you are attempting to reason with — like Marco in the previous case — is still struggling to understand whether SpongeBob SquarePants is real or not. The child's ability to use high-level reasoning to examine his own behavior is, therefore, quite limited.

If you find that reason and logic work with your child or the children you work with, be grateful. But if you have to use restraint, you must first consider the following points.

- Use restraint only when *everything* else has failed. You should exhaust all other methods. Use the "big kid" descriptor or the brain game. Use persuasive talk, letting the child know that she will be rewarded for returning rapidly to positive behavior, but that she will lose access to privileges or toys for continuing negative behavior. Before using restraint, try removing the child from the room in which she is blowing up, because this may interrupt her tantrum. Do not use restraint until you have tried everything else within reason.
- Do not use restraint as a general technique for bad behavior. It should be reserved only for extreme situations. A child who is tearful and grumpy, pitching a fit on the floor, or screaming because he had to turn off the TV or because he did not expect you to stop at a particular store is not actually harming anyone and is not really out of control. Such children do not need to be restrained. They are throwing the type of tantrum that I refer to as "painfully normal." All kids do this to one extent or another, and we should attempt first to deal with it by using traditional soothing methods, like hugging, holding, and comforting. It is our job as parents to help our children through hard situations and to teach them alternatives to having fits and meltdowns. Remember, the only types of explosions that require restraint are those that lead to someone getting hurt or to some place getting wrecked.
- After any incidence of having to restrain a child, immediately return to trying to use the interventions discussed earlier, such as the big kid program and the brain game, in the hope that the child will ultimately learn to respond to her own frustration and anger with appropriate behavior. After a child regains self-control following a big meltdown or the use of restraint, you should praise her effusively for acting

like a big kid, offer kisses and hugs, or give a round of applause.

- Limit the use of restraint to relatively young children. It is rarely necessary with children past kindergarten age, as children age six and up typically have the cognitive development necessary to respond to the other types of interventions I've discussed.
- If your child is not responding to any of the methods I've covered thus far, make sure that he does not have other issues. Your child may very well be exploding due to an environmental allergy or food sensitivity. He may have a sensory processing disorder or a mood disorder such as depression or bipolar disorder. It is not normal for children to be so touchy and explosive that they repeatedly assault others, and it is important that you read and consider all of the other possible causes.

Once you have determined that restraint is absolutely necessary, there are several ways to restrain a young child who is hitting you or others or destroying the environment. Applying the "less is best" type of logic, it is perfectly fine to simply wrap your arms around the child, hold him in your lap, and coo and whisper to him that everything will be OK. This is my favorite technique for interrupting a small child's tantrum, and while it is perhaps counterintuitive, I have seen it work miracles with out-of-control children in my office. Whispering to a child who is screaming can have an almost magical effect, as can rocking the child. In many cases, the child will not even realize that he has been restrained. The point to remember is that when a child's behavior is out of control, all of his internal mechanisms are upset. Soothing the child helps him to regain control in a way that yelling or punishing him never can.

Another technique is to simply "herd" the child around the room. When a child is in the midst of a full-tilt meltdown and you move toward her, she will automatically move away from you in most cases. Use your body to block her access to lamps and table-tops, and don't allow her to stop in any one place for very long. If at all possible, herd her out into a secure outdoor play area and let her walk it off. At some point, the combination of high emotions and movement will simply wear the child out, and you can then use more soothing techniques to help the child regain control.

Things to Remember When Working with an Explosive Child

You now know how to recognize road map meltdowns and transition tantrums. There are other causes of explosive behavior in children, and I will cover them in the following chapters. If, after having read about all of the other causes, you come to the conclusion that your child (or a child you work with as a teacher, physician, or mental health professional) is exploding because of road map and transition issues, always remember the following points in planning your interventions.

- Children with road map and transition issues do not explode on purpose or to be oppositional or defiant. They are, instead, reacting to events external to themselves that they did not expect.
- Children with road map and transition issues are by their very nature exquisitely sensitive to unexpected events, changes, surprises, and transitions. They are sensitive to such events in much the same way that some people have an unexplainable phobia of snakes or bats or spiders. Such phobic reactions are automatic and not under their immediate control.
- Children who explode due to road map and transition issues are as unaware of their impact on others at the moment of exploding as is a person who jumps or screams or flees

when he or she sees a snake. From their point of view, they are reacting to something that is threatening their sense of safety and comfort. They are not trying to defy you or challenge your power when you tell them to calm down, although their arguing can make it seem so.

- Harsh punishments and scolding ultimately won't do anything to change the behavior of children with road map and transition issues, because punishment does nothing to treat the underlying causes of their behavior. These causes include their oversensitivity to unexpected events and changes and their irrational sense that what they think is going to happen is the only thing that can or will happen.
- You are unlikely to talk children out of exploding, although there is much to be said for listening sensitively to children when they attempt to tell you how they feel when they encounter unexpected events and transitions. The most direct way to help them not to explode is to have them frequently face the situations that make them explode, so that they can learn to respond in a more rational manner. If left on their own, they will do their best to avoid these situations, which will ensure that they will never learn how to deal with them and will continue to explode whenever faced with them. It is the avoiding and exploding cycle that leads parents to walk on eggshells with these kids, hoping that the explosions will somehow go away.
- Explosive children need the clearheaded guidance and feedback of parents and other concerned adults, regardless of how vigorously they protest that they don't want help from anyone. It is the adults' job to establish guidelines for what is acceptable behavior and what is not.
- You must remain relentlessly positive with explosive children, letting them know that you have great faith in their ability to learn new ways of responding to the situations that make them blow up. Remember, they are probably used

to being yelled at or punished because of their behavior, and they may think that talking to you is going to lead to even more punishment — this is why they keep their defenses up. They are also likely to believe that even if they try hard, they are bound to fail. Tell them in the friendliest way possible that change is necessary and not optional, but that you will be their coach and cheerleader, and you will make sure their hard work is rewarded with some bigtime fun.

I urge you not to stop reading now and begin to treat your child for road map and transition issues. In the following chapters, you will learn that when it comes to children, a complex view of what is driving their behavior will serve you much better than a simple, single-cause explanation, as seductive and inviting as such explanations may be.

3

MY ALLERGIES ARE AFFECTING THE WAY I FEEL AND BEHAVE

*

MY OLDEST SON is allergic to milk, wheat, and corn, as well as to dust and timothy grass. His dust and grass allergies made themselves known early in his life with a chronic stuffy nose and dark circles under his eyes, but his food allergies were another story. Debilitating headaches and fatigue, unexplained rashes, gastrointestinal problems, recurrent sinus infections, and chronic strep throat were difficult to make sense of. Well-meaning doctor after doctor sent him for tests, and each test came back negative for anything that would explain his symptoms.

In that intuitive way that mothers often have, my wife always suspected that additional, undiagnosed allergies were somehow to blame, but when she visited one of the most well-respected allergists in our area, the doctor told her that allergies could not possibly account for the myriad symptoms our son was experiencing. "What about food allergies?" my wife asked. "Could you test him for that?" The doctor shook her head decisively. "If he was breaking out in hives or having difficulty breathing or something of that nature, I would test him," she said. "But I don't believe he has food allergies."

While our son's condition continued to worsen, my wife and I continued our own search for answers. It took a number of years, but my wife's intuition proved to be correct. We discovered, after doing food elimination diets and consulting with another allergist whose own children had food allergies, that it was indeed the very foods our son was eating each day that were making him sick. And once we finally discovered which foods those were and removed them from his diet, his symptoms began to disappear, almost like magic. I am happy to report that he is currently doing beautifully in college and living a happy and productive life. He has learned that he can eat the offending foods now and then with no side effects, and he tries to maintain a healthy, preservative-free diet.

Although my son did not have the degree of explosiveness that I am writing about in this book (he never displayed behavioral problems in school or in public), he was certainly at times explosive and irritable at home. This would usually occur during one of his episodes of fatigue. I remember going into his bedroom one evening and seeing him propping his eyes open with his fingers so that he could complete his homework. His occasional explosive and irritable behavior was certainly understandable to us, his parents. How could he *not* be explosive and irritable, given the symptoms he faced?

In that uncanny way that life has of teaching us lessons, my son's experiences with allergies have taught me a thing or two about working with children, particularly irritable and explosive children who also have allergies. Now I find myself as curious about their physical symptoms as their behavioral symptoms, knowing from firsthand experience that explosive behavior and allergies can be remarkably interconnected.

The fact is, a surprising percentage of my youngest exploders — particularly those in the three- to six-year-old range — have allergies of some sort. A recent informal review of these children's records suggests that this percentage easily exceeds 50 percent. While I understand that this is far from a scientific survey, it is nonetheless an astonishing statistic, and one that I cannot easily ignore.

The research done on asthma sufferers, perhaps the most extensively studied group of children with allergies, can be brought to bear on this subject. Estimates of the number of American children who suffer from asthma run as high as 12 percent, with the most common form being allergic asthma, which means that the breathing difficulties stem from exposure to things such as dust, pets, or foods. While most readers have some working knowledge of asthma and its breathing complications, I suspect that few are aware of the startling number of psychological and behavioral issues that often accompany it.

A review of several important studies, one of which was funded by the U.S. Department of Health and Human Services, indicates that children with a minor form of asthma are more than one and a half times more likely to display behavioral and conduct problems than children without asthma, children with moderate asthma are three times more likely to display these problems, and children with severe asthma are more than four times more likely to display conduct and behavioral problems. In addition, children with moderate asthma are at twice the risk for displaying learning disabilities, and those with severe asthma are at more than three times the risk. Finally, children with severe asthma are four times more likely than their nonasthmatic peers to need counseling for emotional, developmental, or behavioral problems. Data of this sort leaves us with the clear impression that ignoring the connection between physical health and emotional health is something we do at our own peril or the peril of our children.

When new patients come into my office, their parents are asked to fill out a symptoms checklist. It never ceases to amaze me how, along with check marks next to frequent tantrums, irritability, mood swings, anxiety, attention problems, and hyperactivity, there are check marks next to chronic runny nose, chronic congestion, frequent headaches, frequent stomachaches, frequent ear infections, asthma, fatigue, and dark circles under the eyes. While some of these children have already been formally diagnosed with and treated for asthma and/or allergies to things like dust and pollen, a surprising number have not. And it is the rare child who has been diagnosed with a food allergy, though interestingly, many times the mother has an intuitive sense, as my wife did, that there could be a connection between food and her child's behavior.

Whether allergies are actually a primary cause of behavior problems or whether they simply contribute to the overall load of stress that will push a child over the edge and into depression, anxiety, hyperactivity, inattention, or explosive behavior is a question I can't answer — a question that deserves a great deal more research by both allergists and psychologists. But the lack of a definitive answer doesn't preclude the commonsense notion that when a child can't breathe properly, has pain or hearing loss from constant ear infections, has an immune system that is tired or weakened from battling pollen, dust, or perhaps even the daily exposure to a food allergy, and, on top of that, has to deal with school and social pressures, he is bound to be irritable and explosive. Just think about how we, as adults, are more likely to explode over something insignificant when we have a cold. Many children who are battling environmental allergies and/or food allergies are riding the edge of an explosion on a daily basis.

Unfortunately, I find that many parents seem to downplay their child's allergy symptoms. Perhaps it is because they are just so used to the child's symptoms that they no longer pay attention to them. Or perhaps it is because allergies are so common in our culture that parents regard them as almost normal. Or maybe it is because young children often don't complain about their symptoms. Some children are, in fact, so used to feeling bad that they don't know what it's like to feel good. They are incapable of saying, "Mommy, my ears feel plugged up every time I pet the cat," or "Mommy, the dust mites in my bed make me tired and irritable," or "Mommy, every time I eat corn flakes and milk, I want to hit somebody."

I'm sure I will never forget the thin six-year-old boy who came to my office because his school didn't know what to do with him. He was hyperactive, explosive, and uncontrollable, and the school wanted me to conduct an ADHD test before they placed him in an alternative educational setting. The boy was virtually uncooperative in taking the test. He cried when asked to answer a simple question. He moaned and groaned and fidgeted. He rolled himself up into a ball in the chair and simply refused to participate. From time to time, he would get up and walk over to the window to check for his mother's car. At first I thought he was suffering from abandonment fears—that he was missing his mother. But when she finally did come, he ran out of my office and into the waiting room and, without any greeting at all, immediately began to demand candy. When she told him that she did not have any candy, he kicked her in the shin and demanded candy again. When she told him, in an embarrassed tone of voice—after all, he was doing this in front of a waiting room full of people—that she didn't have any candy, not one single piece, he grabbed hold of a strand of her very long hair and yanked it. This little boy seemed completely unable to contain himself. He then went so far as to demand candy from my office manager, and when she told him that she didn't have any either, he yanked his mother's hair again, enough to bring tears to her eyes.

"Go get some candy right now," he demanded of his mother. And then, as if suddenly realizing that another tactic might be more effective, he looked at her with a sad face and began to beg, *"Please . . . please . . ."*

I informed his mother that I was unable to complete the test, and I suggested that before we give it another try, she come in for an appointment by herself so that we could discuss her son's behavior at greater length. She seemed defensive. "I know you're going to say I shouldn't give him candy, but you see what happens. When I try to get him to eat good food, he just won't eat it. He just wants sugary things. He wants candy and cookies. Sometimes he'll eat hamburgers or French fries or pizza, but that's about all the regular food I can get him to eat. But I don't understand it, because my other kids pretty much eat the same things, and *they* don't act this way. Besides, my son's other doctor said it could be ADHD, so that's why I'm here. I just want my son to try some medicine to see if that helps. I just need something that will work quickly, because the school is constantly calling me at work to come get him, and I'm about to lose my job."

I tried to convince the mother that it would be a better idea to rule out all the other possible causes of his behavior before diagnosing her son with ADHD and putting him on medication, but she didn't want to hear it. She did not show up for her next appointment, and I never found out what happened to her son.

It may be tempting to conclude that this boy was just a brat, throwing a tantrum because he did not get his way, or to go directly to the ADHD diagnosis. But in my opinion, there was something else going on. He displayed a frightening, almost pathological need for candy that seemed to overshadow everything else around him. It certainly prevented him from concentrating during my evaluation of him, and he was completely oblivious to the scene he was making in the waiting room. Was he hyperglycemic or hypoglycemic due to the amount of sugar he was consuming, or was he sensitive to some ingredient in the candy that made him crave it so?

Meet Timothy

Explosive behavior that is either caused or exacerbated by foods and other allergies can look just like the explosive behavior you see in children with road map issues, ADHD, depression, or anxiety. In fact, it is possible that children with allergy-related explosions and behavior problems have been misdiagnosed with ADHD, oppositional defiant disorder, or bipolar disorder by the time they get to my office.

Take Timothy, for instance. Tim was five when he came to my office with his mother and baby sister, who was still in a stroller.

His mother looked tired and frazzled, as the baby was crying and the little boy was whining and pulling on her skirt. One of the first things I noticed about Tim were the dark circles under his sunken eyes and the way his nostrils seemed to flare in and out, as if he was having trouble breathing. He was absent the happy-go-lucky look that a boy his age should have and instead looked like a child who had a bad case of a cold or the flu. His mother was close to tears as she tried to comfort her baby while telling me about her son, who had recently been given a tentative diagnosis of childhood bipolar disorder. He had been kicked out of three daycare centers in rapid succession due to his explosive episodes of yelling and hitting and biting the teachers and other children. He attended a private kindergarten and was about to be kicked out of that, too. At home, it was like walking on eggshells with him. One minute he was fine, and the next minute he was out of control.

When I pointed out that many of the symptoms she had checked off on the intake sheet were allergy- and food sensitivity–related symptoms, her eyes lit up, and she became much more animated. It was as if, instinctively, she knew that we were onto something important in regard to her son's behavior. She already knew that he had allergies to dust and pollen, but she suspected foods as well. In fact, she expressed a great deal of frustration over the fact that she had only recently tried to talk about these issues with her child's doctor, but he had not taken her concerns seriously and had written out a referral to another psychologist, who had concluded that her child was probably exhibiting the beginning stages of bipolar disorder.

But Tim's mother decided that she would not consider putting him on any medication until a broader view of why he acted the way he did was taken. Since there is a good deal of literature indicating that children who have the more common environmental allergies are also prone to food allergies, I encouraged Tim's mother to hold off on both medical and behavioral strategies and to make an appointment with an allergist in our area who believes strongly that there is a relationship between allergies and behavior. She was thrilled to do so and left with a smile and a hopeful look on her face.

When Tim's mother came back about six weeks later, she was smiling from ear to ear. The allergist had tested and diagnosed Tim with allergies to corn, wheat, and eggs. By eliminating these things from her son's diet, she found that the horrible mood swings and tantrums that had plagued him had greatly decreased. Tim's mother also later discovered that he had a marked sensitivity to boxed fruit drinks with coloring in them, which she now refers to as "liquid crazy." As if that wasn't enough, in the process of reworking the way her son ate, she noticed that her baby was also much better on soy milk—not nearly as much crying, fretful behavior, and diaper rashes. She had been able to take Tim to an all-day family reunion out of town, where his behavior had been wonderful. He was, in many ways, no longer the same boy who had been hitting and biting, kicking and thrashing about at home and at school.

I wish I could tell you that all cases work out this magnificently, but of course they don't. Some children's behavior problems are due to other reasons, but cases such as Tim's do hold out hope for all families that something might be gained by stretching our thinking about what is going on with our children.

Fortunately, allergies to things such as dust, pets, mold, grass, and pollen can be easily tested for and pretty well managed with medication and allergy shots. I strongly encourage parents of explosive children to eliminate these stressors, if they exist, from the mix of things. Since these traditional allergies are reasonably well understood by the general public and are treatable, I am not going to spend more time discussing them in this chapter. Instead, I'm going to concentrate on food allergies, which are less well understood but are, from my perspective, remarkably important when it comes to tracking down the sources of explosive behavior.

The Controversy Surrounding Food Allergies

> A vegetable or animal food eaten by a human being . . . consists of tens of thousands of substances of different kinds. The great majority of these substances might serve as antigens, sensitizing some people. Some allergies involve the brain in such a way that exposure to the particular allergen results in peculiarities of behavior.
>
> —LINUS PAULING, two-time Nobel Prize winner

I would be remiss if I did not tell you that the idea that there is a relationship between food allergies and behavior is controversial among allergists and physicians. But once you begin to push your thinking, why is it easier to believe that mold, dust, and pollen cause runny noses, congestion, and rashes than it is to believe that milk causes a child to fall asleep in school two hours after eating cereal that morning, or that a cherry juice box at lunch causes a child to become hyperactive that afternoon, or that corn chips cause a child to lose control of himself and kick and spit at his teacher?

Many allergists believe that the term "food allergy" should be reserved only for events in which contact with a certain food or substance results in immediate and readily observable symptoms such as anaphylactic shock, hives, diarrhea, or difficulty breathing, all of which are called IgE reactions. (IgE stands for immunoglobulin E, a class of antibodies responsible for some allergic reactions.) The position of this camp is that there is inadequate scientific evidence (meaning evidence from large, controlled studies) that foods can actually be the cause of behavioral and psychological problems.

Other allergists believe that this traditional viewpoint is too limited. They maintain that there are flaws in some of the large studies that have not found a link between food and behavior (for instance, that the children were not given a large enough dose of the allergen). They believe that in addition to the immediate, readily observable physical symptoms of food allergies, there are delayed symptoms (IgG, or immunoglobulin G, reactions) that can affect any part of the body, including the central nervous system. They base their beliefs not so much on large studies but on observing individual children's responses to foods. They write about responses that occur anywhere from half an hour to several days after eating a certain food: irritability, depression, anxiety, hyperactivity, disruptions in the ability to concentrate, and defiant and explosive behavior.

According to Doris Rapp, one of the first allergists (along with Benjamin Feingold, who though currently out of public favor deserves credit for his pioneering examination of the impact of additives and preservatives on the behavior of children) to bring this issue to the attention of the public, there are additional reasons why delayed food allergies are not being diagnosed. In her bestselling book *Is This Your Child?* Rapp explains that some children with behavioral problems caused by foods do not show any of the traditional symptoms of allergies (congestion, sneezing, rashes), and thus their doctors will not (and in my opinion, understandably so) suggest testing. To make matters more complicated, formal testing for these kinds of food allergies can be quite tricky, because the tests themselves are not foolproof and can result in false positives and false negatives. But of course, just because a test for an illness is not foolproof does not mean that the illness does not exist.

In addition to all of the above, delayed food allergies can be difficult for doctors to diagnose because they are often so variable and overlapping. For instance, one day a child may respond horribly to a glass of milk, and the next day the same amount of milk may provoke symptoms that are almost unnoticeable. How can this be? Rapp beautifully describes this phenomenon by comparing a child to a barrel that gets filled up with all kinds of stressors: mold, dust, cat dander, grass, viruses, bacteria, bullies at school, parents who argue frequently, food allergies and sensitivities, and so on. On a day that the milk reaction is really bad, the allergic child may also have been exposed to lots of dust, the cat who slept in her bed, and the bully on the bus, thus overflowing her barrel. By contrast, on a day that the milk provokes only a mild reaction, the child's barrel may have contained fewer stressors, leaving her room to adapt.

Another complication is that delayed allergies are often to foods that a child eats every day. In fact, children actually seem to crave these particular foods, much like an alcoholic craves alcohol. I know of a girl who woke up in the middle of the night craving milk, for example. So did her mother. They both thought it was normal to wake up craving milk. I met another girl with bright pink cheeks who couldn't live without corn flakes for breakfast, lunch, and dinner. Each time a child ingests the problem food, he or she has a temporary sense of relief. As the food leaves the system, the need for it increases again. The cycle continues, with the child's behavior and emotions swinging this way and that.

Finally, as has already been touched upon, behavioral reactions may not appear immediately after exposure, sometimes taking hours before they become apparent. Delayed symptoms such as bed-wetting or fretful sleep patterns, for instance, may occur long after eating a food. Because of this time lag, it is difficult to associate the offending substance with the resulting behavior.

All of this brings me to the critical role that parents have in determining whether a child has food allergies. Parents know their child's behavior better than anyone and have the necessary ability and concern to observe the fluctuations of the child's behavior over long periods of time after eating various foods. Parents are able to take into account all of the variables that can make the diagnosis of food allergies tricky. Tricky, but certainly not impossible!

I am reminded here of one of my little patients whose primary caregivers were his grandparents. These fine people were unwilling to leave any stone unturned in an effort to find out why their grandson was so touchy and irritable, tired one minute and climbing the walls the next. Since he had a sandpapery rash on his cheeks, I suggested that they visit an allergist. After testing, they discovered that he was allergic to several foods, primarily corn. (These days, corn is in almost everything imaginable in the form of corn syrup and cornstarch.) The payoff for them has been considerable. As his grandmother said, "Just knowing *why* he behaves the way he does helps so much in how we deal with our grandson." She was amazed that they could always trace his out-of-control, explosive behavior to something he had accidentally ingested that had corn in it.

So whom should you believe if, after reading this chapter, you suspect that your child may have a food allergy that is impacting his or her behavior? While I am not saying that you should completely dismiss some of the large studies that say there is not enough evidence to support the idea that food can affect behavior, I would also caution you to keep in mind that experimental design is a complex field. Large studies involve pooling data and looking at averages. This averaging makes sense because we would not want the results of a study to be unduly influenced by the unusual scores of just a few individuals, known as "statistical outliers." But we tend to forget that these outliers are actual children and that something of vast importance might be learned by mulling over why their scores deviate so much from the average. Such children represent the trees, not the forest. Such children may be the very children I am writing about in this book. So while it is smart to be aware of what the large studies have found, we must not be blinded by them.

Indications of a Food Allergy

There are more symptoms associated with delayed food allergies in children than you might expect. Some of the more common symptoms that I have noticed in the children I work with are listed here. Examine the list to determine whether any of these symptoms apply to your child. You should be particularly suspect if your child exhibits both physical and behavioral symptoms.

Dark circles under eyes
Rosy cheeks
Stuffy or runny nose
Skin rashes
Glassy eyes
Digestive problems
Headaches
Numerous ear and sinus infections
Colic as an infant
Bed-wetting
Excessive drooling
Depression
Irritability and mood swings
Sleep problems
Temper tantrums
Fatigue, sometimes extreme
Hyperactivity or extreme talkativeness
Lots of crying and whining spells
Craving particular foods
Learning disabilities
Inattentiveness

If you recognize a number of symptoms in the list, you will need to begin questioning the foods that your child is eating. While it is possible for a child to be allergic or sensitive to almost any food or food additive, the following foods seem to be some of the main delayed allergy offenders.

Additives (food dyes and colorings, BHA, BHT, gums, lecithin, MSG, sweeteners, benzoates, nitrates, sulfites)
Aspartame (found in many sugar-free products)
Corn (found in corn syrup, cornstarch, confectioners' sugar, bread, corn chips)

Eggs (found in many products, including baked goods)
Food dyes (found in candies, fruit drinks, vitamins)
Milk (including yogurt, cheese, sour cream, ice cream, butter, margarine)
Soy (found in many processed foods and baked goods)
Sugar (found in many products, including baked goods)
Wheat (found in breads, cereals, baked goods, hot dogs, lunch meats)

Many other foods and drinks may be contributing to your child's explosive behavior. In fact, any substance can be the culprit, including things as innocuous as cinnamon, squash, and bananas. And keep in mind, as I indicated earlier, that there may be more than one food at issue. For instance, a child may be sensitive to milk *and* wheat.

The Food Elimination Diet

So how do you determine whether your child is having a delayed reaction to a particular food? As I mentioned previously, food allergy testing, especially for delayed reactions, does not appear to be an exact science. Many allergists recommend a food diary as a first step in the process, whereby the parents use the diary to chart their child's food intake and behavior for several weeks. This means keeping track of everything the child eats and drinks. I suggest purchasing a special notebook for your food diary. Make sure to leave enough room to chart your observations and suspicions, and try to be relatively neat in your presentation of material so that an allergist can make sense of it later if needed.

Each day for two weeks, write down every single thing your child eats and drinks for breakfast. This should include specifics, such as how many glasses of milk or how many pieces of toast. Pay attention to any behavioral or physical changes you see after the meal. If there are no changes, indicate that as well. Do the same for lunch and dinner. As you continue on in this manner, you may see patterns emerging. Pay attention to the foods you see appearing over and over, because quite often those are precisely the foods your child may be sensitive to. Also, pay particular attention to the foods your child is demanding, as there is a tendency to crave what you are sensitive to. Maybe it's juice boxes, peanut butter, or yogurt. These would all be considered suspect foods if your child craves them.

Examine the ingredients in these foods. For instance, most yogurt contains not only milk but corn syrup as well. In fact, you may be surprised to learn that corn and wheat appear, in one form or another, in most of the boxed, canned, and prepared foods your child eats. You may find that your child is calm before breakfast, but after a meal of cereal with milk and sugar, he becomes irritable. Suspect each item, the cereal itself, milk, sugar, or perhaps even a food coloring or additive in the cereal, then test each one individually.

You may want to make your child's teacher aware of what you are doing and ask the teacher if he or she sees any pattern in your child's behavior. Is the child worse in the morning or after lunch, for instance? Perhaps you can even provide the teacher with a form that he or she can fill out at the end of each day. You may be surprised at how cooperative the teacher will be, as he or she also is invested in keeping your child calm. An added advantage is that some teachers will cut a child a bit more slack if they know that an effort is being made at home to deal with the behavior problem.

After narrowing down a list of suspect foods, it is time to try the elimination diet. Many allergists consider this the "gold standard" test. It works like this: Taking each suspect food one at a time *(Note: Do not test foods that you already know cause serious reactions),* do not include it in your child's diet in any form for four full days. (Although the number of days varies, many experts seem to agree on the four-day period of abstinence.) For instance, if you are testing milk, the child should have no milk, cheese, yogurt, ice cream, or other dairy product for four full days. Remember that many packaged foods have milk as an ingredient in the form of whey or casein, so read those ingredient labels! After the fourth day, reintroduce the food in an ample amount when you will be able to monitor your child's behavior. For instance, if you are testing for milk, give the child a large glass of milk. If you are testing for eggs, give the child a plate of several scrambled eggs. Record your observations in the food diary.

After four days without the food, any symptoms will be more apparent than usual when you reintroduce the food. Sometimes there is an immediate result: sneezing, breaking out in hives, red cheeks, and so on. Sometimes the symptoms appear between ten minutes and two hours later in the form of hyperactivity, irritability, mood swings, extreme fatigue, headache, and the like. Sometimes the symptoms appear that night in the form of nightmares, bed-wetting, or diarrhea. If your child does not display marked symptoms during the next twenty-four hours, you can probably conclude that the food is not causing her problems.

What to Do if Your Child Has an Unexpected Strong Reaction to a Food

Remember, do not test any food that you already know causes strong reactions in your child. Reactions such as tightness in the throat, inability to breathe, wheezing, swelling of the tongue, hoarseness, or blue lips or fingernails indicate that you need to seek medical attention immediately.

Treatment Options

If your child is reacting to one or more foods, you may simply want to eliminate them from his diet for several weeks and observe his behavior. Consulting an allergist who is open to talking about the impact that these foods seem to have on your child can also be very useful. The allergist can help confirm your suspicions and suggest a new diet for your child.

How can you tell whether a particular allergist will be a good one to work with? Simply call his or her office and tell the person who answers the phone that your child is experiencing some behavior problems and/or other allergy symptoms and see what she says. If the person responds as if this is business as usual, great! If the person acts as if this is an unusual request or indicates that food testing can be done only if traditional allergy symptoms such as sneezing and a runny nose are present, say thank you very much and call another doctor. You may also simply ask the question point-blank: "Does Dr. Smith have a lot of experience testing for IgG food allergies that result in behavioral problems in children?"

Of course, it is not easy to keep a child away from foods such as milk, wheat, eggs, and corn. Some people believe that children can outgrow certain allergies but that allergies to things such as peanuts and shellfish will never go away. Food allergy experts James Braly and Patrick Holford, authors of *Hidden Food Allergies,* feel that it may be possible in some cases for children to eat problem foods after staying away from them for three to six months. You should reintroduce such foods very carefully, however, while checking for reactions. If there are no reactions, you may "rotate" the foods in the child's diet, which means that these foods cannot be eaten any more frequently than every three days. *Note: This does not hold true for foods that provoke serious reactions. You should never attempt to reintroduce those foods into your child's diet unless she is under a doctor's supervision.*

So there is hope that your child may not be deprived of his favorite foods forever, and I strongly encourage you to do much more extensive research on this subject than appears in this chapter. There are many books on both immediate and delayed food allergies, and there are many allergists (including pediatric allergists) who have a keen interest in the behavior connection with food. Also be aware that the allergy-free food industry is booming. You may be surprised at the wealth of allergen-free foods at your grocery store and on the Internet.

Disciplining a Child with Allergies

How do you discipline an explosive child who has allergies? If the allergies are to dust, pollen, or the cat, for instance, using the proper medication or getting allergy shots and attempting to rid the child's environment of the stressors should go a long way toward helping you reason with your child. If your child is completely out of control due to a food, you cannot hold the child fully responsible for that behavior, particularly if she is very young. It is simply impossible to reason with many children who are in the midst of a reaction to a food. They are often irritable and explosive. The important thing is to try to remain calm and soothing toward the child. Of course, once you become convinced that a particular food provokes a negative reaction, that food must be eliminated.

Do not expect that all of your child's negative behavior patterns, such as whining and complaining, will disappear immediately after you remove the problem food. Your child should, however, be much easier to discipline and reason with. Depending on the child's age, it is important to explain the connection between food and behavior and to let him know that he should begin to feel better with the elimination of that food.

Finally, many explosive children who are affected by foods have been getting in trouble at home and at school all their lives for reasons beyond their control. Often they feel that they are "the bad kid of the family," as one child recently told me. In cases like this, it may help to take your child to a psychologist who can help her regain her sense of self-worth.

It is important to remember that not all explosive behavior problems are caused by allergies and not all allergies result in explosive behavior. So even if you find yourself interested in and excited about the prospect of going to an allergist or trying the food elimination diet, you should continue to read on in this book. A number of other causes of explosive behavior are yet to be discussed in

Statements from Parents Regarding Food Allergies and Behavior

We have seen our son's behavior change 180 degrees. We call it the miracle diet. We now know how much his behavior is affected by the foods he eats. We know that if he has Teddy Grahams for a snack, we'll have to peel him off the ceiling a few hours later. We had no idea that he was experiencing a sensitivity to such a degree until we did the elimination diet . . . Prior to the diet, he was impulsive, couldn't sit still, had trouble sleeping, bowel habits were disrupted, he experienced bed-wetting, fits of anger and rage followed by crying, dark circles under his eyes, and trouble concentrating. By following his new food plan (we worked with an allergist who understands the diet-behavior connection), our son is a different child. It has been a lifesaver for all of us.

Our grandson arrived to live with us at three and a half. Although we loved him dearly, he was much more than we anticipated. He threw temper tantrums, constantly testing our limits and boundaries, and was . . . in perpetual motion. We did behavior modification and use of consequences and had some success, but six months later we began to experiment with diet, and his behavior changed dramatically. He is now much easier to manage. He now is a typical four-year-old boy—not perfect, but manageable. Diet has worked wonders for this little boy.

depth in the remaining chapters. However, the importance of determining whether your exploding child does have allergies cannot be underestimated. Not only can allergic reactions manifest as explosive behavior, anxiety, depression, attention issues, and oppositional behavior, but they also can occur in addition to these issues, making them substantially worse. By dealing with allergies as part of your child's overall care, you stand a good chance of being able to deal with the other issues more easily.

4

I DON'T LIKE RULES!

*

I INDICATED IN CHAPTER 1 that there is a great deal of confusion among parents, teachers, physicians, and mental health professionals about the terms "defiant" (also known as "oppositional") and "explosive." My main purpose in this chapter is to attempt to clarify the issue.

First, let me offer a logical proposition: all children who are explosive are not defiant, and all children who are defiant are not explosive. But the fact that these two categories of childhood behavior can and do overlap is what causes general confusion. The trend among many of my colleagues today is to say that all children who chronically explode are defiant children. This is wrong, of course, as we saw with Steven and Henry in chapter 1.

This is an honest confusion. It causes me, however, to have to put these terms under even more magnification so that we can clearly see the differences between defiant children and their peers who explode for other reasons. It is useful at this juncture to compare defiant children to children who explode due to road map and transition issues, given that the road map children are so commonly mistaken to be defiant children. However, it is also prudent to keep in mind that any child who explodes frequently stands a good chance of being misdiagnosed as defiant. This goes for the children we have examined so far, including those with food sensitivities and environmental allergies, and the others we have yet to examine. Truly you need to be able to tell who is defiant and who isn't, and the faster you can do this in your contact with them, the better.

Every exploding child is overly sensitive to something—this is why he or she explodes in the first place. Defiant children are exquisitely sensitive to the difference in power between children and adults. Their defiant behavior and explosions are part of their attempt to close the power gap.

Let's look at Roland, who had just turned four when I met him. His teacher sent me this note:

> When he becomes angry at me he balls his fist up and punches at me. His favorite sport is sneaking up behind me and trying to trip me to embarrass me. When I put him in time out he spits at me and laughs at me until I let him out. If I don't let him out of time out fast enough, he begins to throw chairs and turn over tables.

I want you to focus on two aspects of Roland's behavior, because they are central to being able to identify children who are defiant. The first is his willingness to do battle with the adults. Defiant children are known for their arguing, their refusal to comply with even simple requests, and their willingness to show you that you cannot make them do anything. Roland's mother will tell you that if you say to him, "You have to breathe," he will hold his breath until he passes out.

The second aspect of Roland's behavior that I want you to consider is his drive to get what he wants, when he wants it. He is, in all truth, as relentless as gravity. He argues, he demands, he threatens, and it is when his demands ultimately go unmet that he explodes. His mother refers to his explosions as his method of punishing you when he does not get what he wants. Think of his explosions as retribution explosions and you get the point.

So, let's compare how a defiant child's explosion feels to the observer, versus how a child with road map and transition issues explodes.

- A road map explosion is unplanned, often frantic, and seems instantaneous because the child's sense of safety has been threatened and he is on red alert—a flip of the switch type of event. A defiant child like Roland typically works on you first in an attempt to get what he wants, watching you all along the way to see what you are going to do. When you ultimately frustrate him long enough, he explodes to get you back.

- Most kids who explode over road map, transition, and anxiety-related issues would like to be able to change because they do not like the way they feel after they explode. Once they reach the six- and seven-year-old range, they become aware that their peers avoid them (they often complain that "nobody likes me at school"), although they have little insight that this is because they explode, are too easily frustrated, are often tense and nervous, and simply aren't that much fun. As they grow older, they sometimes begin to realize that other kids easily do things that they are hesitant or fearful to do and that others generally roll with events with less effort. By contrast, oppositional kids see themselves as the freedom fighters of the kid world. They do not really want to change because they believe themselves to be in a righteous struggle with the adult world over power and control. They are often physically and emotionally vigorous, and as they approach puberty they are often popular with their peers due to their bravery against adults. It is not uncommon for oppositional kids to tease the kids who are sensitive to unexpected events to make them blow up for entertainment.

- Children with road map issues are often full of remorse and regret over their explosions, particularly the young ones, and they will seek forgiveness. At the very least, they will admit that the way they acted was wrong. Defiant kids tend to believe that they have little to apologize for and will argue this point relentlessly.

- Defiant children can be oppositional more frequently than road map children can explode. Being oppositional does not wear you out nearly as much as exploding does. In many respects, there are only so many times a day a child can explode, whereas there is virtually no limit to the number of times an oppositional child can be oppositional.

- As defiant children age, they tend to get more attitudinal, with this peaking just before they are old enough to get their learner's permit to drive. (It is amazing how a bad attitude diminishes once you make your child aware that he stands no chance of driving your car.) By contrast, kids with road map issues do not necessarily come across as attitudinal. They can be soft-spoken and somewhat shy around others, although this is not a hard and fast rule. They often remain passive until they are faced with an unexpected event or transition, at which point the switch gets flipped and off they go.

- Children with road map and transition issues seek routine in all aspects of their lives. When young, they may be extremely sensitive to when bath time is *supposed* to be, how a hotdog is *supposed* to be cut up, and how many kisses and hugs they are *supposed* to get at bedtime. They desperately want things to stay the same all the time. In comparison, oppositional defiant children adapt to fluctuations in their routines relatively easily.

- Most children from healthy, functioning families are used to a routine, with few deviations day to day. Road map children tend to remain stable when surrounded by healthy routine and sameness. Defiant kids are defiant even when everything in the family is going perfectly, although tensions in the home can certainly make them worse.

- Road map meltdowns and transition tantrums are not in any manner a conscious decision or battle strategy—they are reactions to unanticipated events. Road map kids often hold their emotions in check with a great deal of effort in order to make themselves look calm, but their anxiety over unexpected events or transitions and their safety fears are still ticking like a time bomb in the background. Oppositional, defiant kids spend a great amount of time plotting how to do battle with the powers that be and often don't care about keeping their feelings and emotions in check.
- Children with road map and transition issues may seem as quick as defiant children to say "No!" when you make a request or give an order. However, they do this to preserve their sense of safety, because for them to remain calm and feeling safe, things must unfold as they anticipated. By contrast, defiant children tell you "No!" because they want to establish that they are your coequal in the hierarchy of power and will go to great lengths to prove it to you.

Your ultimate tool in determining whether a young child is explosive due to defiance or explosive due to road map–related issues is to watch closely how she handles unexpected situations.

The Causes of Oppositional Behavior

Now that you have reviewed the differences in explosions, you may still question what the underlying causes of defiant behavior are. In truth, no one knows for sure. My perspective is that it is primarily a personality type, a temperament that a child is born with. It is not caused by the typical parenting mistakes and lapses that we all commit—something that the parents of most oppositional defiant children worry about deeply because they so often see their children's behavior as a reflection of their worth as a parent. I say this because over the years, I have seen far too many oppositional children who were ripping it up at home, but who had brothers or sisters who were quite pleasant to be around. All of the kids were raised in the same family, typically even the same house, with the same rules and standards, yet one turns out one way, and the others turn out another.

These questions about why kids turn out the way they do are certainly interesting, and we get hints from every possible direction about the causes. For example, more inhibited than uninhibited children have blue eyes and a thin frame, whereas more uninhibited children have brown eyes and a robust frame.

Although this points the finger in the direction of genetics, genes do not tell the entire tale. This is particularly true when we are talking about oppositional behavior. We can't ignore a child's internal world—how she thinks—in searching for the causes of oppositional behavior. For example, in comparison to their mild-mannered peers, boys with disruptive behavior are more prone to devise aggressive solutions to their problems with others. They are also less adept at understanding social cues and tend to attribute hostile intent to others when, in fact, none exists.

Facts like these show the immense complexity of human behavior and give us hints of how biological, environmental, and cognitive forces interact to create defiant or explosive behavior. Readers who are seeking an easy explanation for why children explode or act in an oppositional manner will find this disappointing. For others, myself included, such facts only serve to heighten the intrigue of why children do what they do.

When considering why oppositional children act the way they do, it is best to examine their behavior in several contexts. Few oppositional children act the same in every type of environment.

The Defiant Child at Home

For defiant children in the age category addressed in this book, roughly three to ten years old, home is where the biggest and most frequent explosions occur. This is not to say that they never act out at school or in stores, because they obviously do. They are in fact famous for arguing with their teachers from a young age (they argue with anyone whose job it is to be in charge of them). But, as I said, they save their best for those who love them the most. What they display in public is only a fraction of what they let loose at home.

I have met literally hundreds of three-, four-, and five-year-olds who hit their parents, kick doors and walls, and otherwise attempt to destroy their homes, but who are as pleasant and sweet-natured to be around as you could imagine when I see them at my office or happen to bump into them in some other setting. Don't be surprised if your neighbors, friends, and relatives find it hard to believe that your child is defiant.

I have also had many occasions in which a parent videotaped or audiotaped a child in full-blown home meltdown. At my office, one nine-year-old boy, Clay, could have served as the poster child for a happy Irish-American child: bright red hair, freckles, sparkling blue eyes, and a sunny disposition. Yet I watched a tape of him as he kicked in his door and threatened to destroy his mother's video camera if she followed through on her threat to show me the tape of how he acted at home. All of this began after his mother refused to let him stay up late playing video games because he had to get up early for a field trip the next day.

It will be a bit before I get into specific techniques for dealing with a defiant child, but at this point I will say emphatically that home is where the battle lines must be drawn. Home is the first place where a defiant child must face the fact that he is indeed a child and not the equal of his parents or other adults. It is the first place where he must learn to comply with family and societal standards and also learn that refusing to do so will have guaranteed costs. Parents who are unwilling to engage in this battle at home when their child first begins to display oppositional behavior are in the long run not doing anyone, including the child, any favors.

The Defiant Child at School

Preschool, kindergarten, and first-grade teachers will tell you that one of the hallmarks of defiant children is that they are prone to refuse to do what all the other children in the classroom comply with easily, seemingly just for the sake of refusing. They argue with the people in charge of them over insignificant issues such as why they need to stand in line with the other children, why they have to sit during circle time, or how many cookies they should get at snack time. They argue, in actuality, about everything, in an attempt to make their teachers, like their parents, throw their hands up and say, "OK, do it your way!" This is precisely what any defiant child hopes to hear from the adults she is around. It is when you do not say, "OK, do it your way!" that the explosion occurs, in an attempt to force the issue.

As defiant children get older, they often make a show out of their defiance at school by taking on teachers or administrators when it is certain that their peers will be watching. They can be amazingly quick to develop a nonchalant attitude toward teachers, using phrases such as "Whatever" or "So?" to let them know that they couldn't care less what the teacher has to say.

The Defiant Child in Public

The defiant children in this book have yet to reach the point in their development at which they like to parade that middle finger through the streets. Some who are just past ten are beginning to do it. We have all seen the skinny, barely pubescent boys standing outside the mall smoking cigarettes, struggling to look tough, spitting, cursing, and doing whatever else they think will catch the attention of girls or intimidate their more timid male peers. But for the most part, kids who are three to ten are still kids and don't make such a public show of their contempt for the rules.

This is not to say that they will necessarily be enjoyable to take shopping. The parents of these children can tell you plenty of stories of arguing with them in stores or of children having a tantrum or creating a scene when they do not get their way. Again, defiant children do not feel particularly bad or remorseful afterward, given that they see arguing with their parents as a disagreement between coequals.

The Defiant Child and His Peers

As I've hinted earlier, oppositional defiant children run an interesting course as they age. Between kindergarten and about third grade, the other kids often stay away from them, labeling them as "bad kids." The thinking goes something like this: if I'm your friend and you blow up and whack the teacher every day, she might think I'm a bad kid too.

This begins to change in the fourth and fifth grades, and it changes even more dramatically in middle school and high school. Should you doubt this progression, talk to a fourteen-year-old girl and ask her why she chooses "bad boys" over "good boys." The girls in this age group tell me that the "good boys" (meaning smart and/or involved in team sports and/or relatively neat in appearance) are boring. This, of course, is one of the worst things that a preadolescent or adolescent girl can say about any boy who is interested in her.

Is it any wonder, then, that so many boys want to exercise their inner bad selves once they get close to puberty? If you want to see examples of all this, go to any of the websites where preteens post information about themselves. Look at the nicknames they use and the poses they strike in photos. Bad to the bone.

A Conversation with an Oppositional Child

I once worked with a boy who was about ten years old and had taken to hitting his tired, overworked mother and his two younger sisters. He had always been able to get his mother to engage in lengthy arguments with him and had learned that she would back down and let him have his way rather than go through another argument or explosion. Regardless of what she would say to him or ask him to do, his first response would be "Why?" She would then explain why, to which he would invariably respond, "That's stupid." She would take the bait every time. I told her a thousand times to stop explaining herself to him and not to be concerned with whether or not he liked or agreed with her parental positions on various issues. I explained that this was his main ploy for getting her to argue. "You are the what?" I would ask her. "And he is the what?" "I know, I know, I know," she would say. "I'm the mom, and he's the kid."

In my office one day, as she and I were talking about his recent behavior, he tried to go into her purse and get his portable electronic game. She had it in her purse because she knew that I don't allow electronic games in my office. (Kids who use them in the waiting room spend the first twenty minutes in the therapy session answering "I don't know" to everything I ask because of the brain fog the games put them in.) When she would not let him have the game, he drew back his fist. Our interaction went something like this:

ME: Have a seat and calm down. There will be no hitting in my office.

HIM: Why?

ME: Because those are the rules in my office.

HIM: Those are stupid rules.

ME: You are free to think what you want, but those are the rules. Please have a seat.

HIM: Well, suppose I don't want to have a seat?

ME: You are certainly free to stand up the entire session if you'd like. Just remember, there is no hitting of any sort allowed in my office, and you will never be allowed to hit your mother and get away with it.

HIM: I could kick her. Kicking isn't hitting. It's kicking.

ME: Either one will cost you.

HIM: What if I do it anyway?

ME: Then you're guaranteed to end up grounded all weekend and you'll lose your stuff. It's pretty simple.
HIM: What if I hit you?
ME: Like I said, guaranteed boring weekend.

You can see where this was headed. Like most oppositional kids, he was probing, looking for evidence of whether it was safe to go chasing after an oppositional victory or whether he should back off. While you cannot tell it from simply reading my words, my behavior toward him during all of this remained truthful and direct about the consequences he was headed toward should he make a bad decision. He was watching me like a hawk, and it struck me that he did not exactly know what to do with me, because I would not allow him to pull me into a heated argument, which, with defiant children, is the on-ramp toward an explosion.

Preparing Yourself for Working with an Oppositional Child

The first rule you must accept in working with an oppositional child of any age, whether you are a parent, a teacher, or a therapist, is that you cannot take his behavior personally and let it cascade into a yelling, screaming test of wills. Hurt parents, teachers, and therapists sometimes act too forcefully or irrationally, and nothing good comes of the situation. Anytime you get goaded into a screaming match with a child, you have already lost. Heat transports you directly to the defiant child's turf. It puts you exactly where he wants you, because his intent is to push you into a fight. Once you begin to argue, all of his fantasies about defeating adults get engaged, and he will argue with you all day long, and all night as well, inching closer and closer to his explosion as you continue to talk.

Instead of taking it personally when a child is in oppositional mode, you must maintain a calm, straightforward attitude in which you point out the error of the direction in which the child is headed. While doing this, you must also offer her clear alternatives that will help the child to stay out of trouble.

You must use your calm, straightforward manner to convince the child that he or she does not stand a chance of getting any reinforcement or reward out of being oppositional. Forget about bargaining or lecturing. The first tactic deludes the child into thinking that she is your equal and possibly puts her on the road to believing that all adults must bargain with her. The second bores her to the point that all she sees are your lips flapping, because she isn't paying any attention to the words coming out of your mouth.

Gaining Control of a Defiant Child

Let's start with the youngest children who are displaying aspects of defiant behavior, those in the three- to four-and-a-half-year-old range. The reason that I make this particular age split is that children who are just past four and a half can typically be dealt with verbally in a more sophisticated manner than children under four and a half. In all regards, you will do best to know your own child, or the children you work with, and use techniques with the child that he can readily understand.

With this youngest age group, you should split the child's world into the "big" and "little" dimensions, following many of the guidelines discussed in chapter 2. Get used to the idea that you must become a broken record with the child. Given the tendency of oppositional children to try to ignore parents and other adults, you must repeat over and over that the only way to get access to the good stuff is by acting "big." Acting big means no exploding, no outrageous tantrums, no slamming doors or kicking walls or stomping toys, no melting down, no hitting.

While I am always hesitant to punish children who explode due to road map issues and I do my best to avoid it, I have different beliefs regarding defiant children, based on years of contact with them. It is very important for a defiant child to learn early in life that his stubbornness and resistance to parental authority will rapidly result in consequences that he is guaranteed not to like. Do not use repeated warnings and lectures, as these can actually get in the way of a child making the association between negative behaviors and negative consequences.

Many parents are understandably confused about how much to take away and how long to take it away. The ground rule is to take away only as much as is needed to get the child's attention and to keep it for the same amount of time. But you must be willing to get his attention. Consequences for highly negative behavior can be losing their favorite toys and activities for periods ranging from an hour or so to an entire day, depending on the severity of the behavior and how rapidly your child learns to display more acceptable behavior. For example, the only toys that are available to a defiant child who is not operating in the "big guy zone" or the "big girl zone" are objects that will not provide any real entertainment value — two Legos, an old car, or a doll that the child is no longer interested in. If your child turns up his nose and says, "Is this all I get to play with?" you have achieved your goal — you now have his attention.

If this doesn't work, it can be intensified further by going deeper into the child's list of reinforcers. Young children are particularly sensitive to what time they have to go to bed and see it as a marker of their "bigness." If you have the child go to bed an hour earlier because she is not acting big, you will clearly get her attention. Likewise, young children are sensitive and proud about their clothing. Favored shirts, shoes, and pants should always be described as the child's "big kid clothes," something that will have to be relinquished for plainer duds when the child's behavior is not acceptable. Also on the list of things that can be lost are access to favorite snacks, watching TV and videos, going outside, having play dates with friends, and essentially any other activity that you know your child enjoys.

You can use similar but modified techniques with children who are older than four and a half. For example, if you allow your child to watch TV or videos, he will develop a range of favorites, from cartoons to the Weather Channel. Limiting your six-year-old to a Teletubby or Barney video that he can watch on your VCR or DVD player will most likely get his attention: "Sorry. This is all you get to watch until you are acting properly."

When dealing with kids who are nine or ten, I always point out that their loss of privileges is not really a punishment. Instead, it shows them how much they have earned based on their behavior. Taking away privileges is the parent's attempt to let the child know that none of the good stuff is free and access to desired activities and things is directly related to behavior.

Getting your child's attention provides him or her with an opportunity to return to acceptable behavior as soon as possible and teaches the lesson early in life that the best reinforcers are reserved for the best efforts. Many of the older children I work with harbor the odd belief that their marginal behavior and achievements have earned them access to a level of privileges and reinforcers that most parents were raised to believe were reserved for high-performing individuals. This is a generation gap issue if ever there was one. Most of the parents I work with were brought up on the idea that everything is earned. But many of today's children and teens believe that expensive electronic games and cell phones should be theirs simply for the asking. If we allow children to have access to the best stuff during the worst behavior, we are teaching them that their bad behavior should and will be rewarded.

Now We Get to the Good Stuff

While it is important to talk to defiant children about what they will miss out on if they do not act appropriately, it is vitally important—and a whole lot more fun—to be sure to remind them of what they will gain by acting "big" or acting "maturely." (Remember to choose your words carefully, depending on your child's age.) This is where you get to use your sense of humor again, and your sense of fun. Making your child aware of everything that can be gained by dropping the oppositional behavior rarely fails to result in behavior changes if you convince your child that you really mean it. I'll show you how.

I once worked with a nine-year-old girl who threw dramatic tantrums at home when she did not get her way. She had no known problems with road map and transition issues and did not appear to be anxious. Her parents described her as "nine going on thirteen," cagey and manipulative beyond her years, with a strong personality and a keen willingness to take on adults. While she did well in school and had no learning difficulties, she was constantly challenging her teachers with her arguing and her refusal to do anything she did not want to do. All indications were that she exploded as a strategy to get her way when her initial ploys did not work.

When I first met her it seemed to me that she had read that oppozoid manual that many teenagers read: She sat on the couch in my waiting room with her arms crossed, an angry scowl on her face, looking down. She refused to shake hands with me when I greeted her. Once she and her parents were seated in my office, she continued to resist eye contact, but she did make quite a show of rolling her eyes whenever her mother or father said something she did not like. When I tried to engage her in talk, she said, "I don't know."

Keep in mind that this was a child who was said to be quite popular with the other kids in her grade, although she was prone to hang out with the little "alpha female" clique and could be, as her mother put it, "a real snot to the shy girls." She was definitely interested in boys, and one of the first things she opened up about in my office was being mad that she couldn't have a cell phone.

I remained neutral toward her in our first session. I wanted to observe how she interacted with her parents and with me. I concluded that her parents were describing her behavior factually, because I saw the way she treated them and me in my office. It was clear that she was willing to ignore them and to be remarkably rude to anyone she felt had crossed her, myself included.

At our second session, I told her that it was time for us to have a talk (with her parents present) so that she could understand how I intended to work with her and could learn what types of things she could expect to hear me say to her parents. I told her that our discussion would be friendly and honest, and I offered her a soft drink in an attempt to show her that I really did want her to be comfortable. She continued to resist eye contact and refused to interact in a polite manner. I see this often in children who believe that if they are rude enough or won't talk, I will turn to their parents and say, "Sorry, I'm defeated. No more need for contact."

I typically tell oppositional kids who act like this girl that there is both good news and bad news, and I ask them which they want to hear first. In her case, she said she wanted to hear the bad news first, which I told her I thought was a good idea. I promised her that she would not like the bad news, but I asked her to hang in with me because she would be very, very happy with the good news. I told her that I was going to go into the things that her parents could do to get her attention if her behavior did not change. However, I made sure that she understood that I do not really like punishments, that it is my job to teach kids how to act and behave so that they rarely, if ever, have to be punished. I explained that the types of losses I would talk about with her parents would occur only if necessary to get her attention. I told her that these losses could be things such as early bedtime; loss of access to favored possessions and activities; loss of favored clothes, electronics, snacks, desserts, phone and computer privileges, and so on. I told her about the girl I wrote about in *The Defiant Child* who was so stubborn about changing her behavior that her parents had to strip her room completely. When I finished my list of possible losses, I asked her whether she believed that her parents would go this far. She said that she was sure they would, because they were very unhappy with her behavior. I asked her to ask her parents to tell her just how close they were to using drastic measures. When she asked, they responded that they were about a hairsbreadth away.

Once this was out of the way, I told her that it was now time for me to tell everyone about the way I prefer working with kids her age. I explained to her, as I do to most oppositional children, that I knew it would be hard work to change her behavior and that I would never ask a child to work so hard without being rewarded really well for her efforts. (This is the point where all of a sudden the defiant children make eye contact.) I also told her that I was not into little rewards, that I was into big rewards, after which I launched into the types of things I tried to give my own children when they were acting the way they knew they should act.

For example, I reminded her that spring and summer were just around the corner, and I gave her the typical list of activities that she might be able to access through good behavior. I told her that her parents might arrange for her to go to Busch Gardens, a giant amusement park in nearby Williamsburg, Virginia, with several of her friends. Or her mom or dad could pick up her friends and take them all to the movies, where they wouldn't even have to sit by the parent — they could sit several rows away, eating their popcorn and drinking their drinks and having fun being away from the adults. I told her that she and her mother could spend a day shopping at the upscale mall in Norfolk, Virginia, and go to an awesome lunch while they were there.

She was, as are so many oppositional children, surprised and enthralled by the prospect of being treated like this. She admitted that she was acting the way she was toward me because she thought that she was being brought to my office for punishment and was mad about it. She was very aware that her recent behavior toward adults would not cut it.

I jokingly asked her which set of methods she wanted us to use to help her make the changes that her parents believed to be necessary: did she want the method of her parents taking everything away, or did she want to earn all the cool rewards? Her answer was emphatic. She wanted to earn the rewards. She was beaming and excited by the time we finished our talk, obviously engaged by the idea of how to improve her behavior based on the promise, as she put it, of being treated so "bigly."

If you have questions about using big rewards, you are not alone. Many parents tell me that they want their children to change because that is what they should do. They should not have to be bribed to do it. I understand this position and always say that if their children would make changes on the basis of that moral argument, they would not be sitting in my office. Besides, it is the rare nine-year-old who uses this type of reasoning. Instead, kids at this age are stuck in the developmental stage where they make changes primarily to avoid punishment and to gain something. Don't be distressed by this. As kids age, the complexity of their moral reasoning changes, and they begin to think about what type of person they should be.

The reasoning behind my reward system goes like this: Reward and praise are the mechanisms that parents can use to get children to come on board with new behaviors and abandon their older negative behaviors. If you can induce your child to increase the number of positive behaviors that he displays, you will have more opportunities to reward him and praise his positive behaviors. Over time, the positive behaviors will begin to replace the negative behaviors, because the positives are being continually reinforced and the negatives are being met with undesirable consequences. As your child exhibits the positive behaviors in most circumstances, you can begin to ease up on the large, costly reinforcers but maintain the social reinforcers, such as praise, hugs, and high-fives, and an enhanced but relatively inexpensive set of privileges, such as a later bedtime, more individual discretion about phone and computer use, and free access to school and community activities with their friends.

In sum, eliminating the explosive, argumentative behavior of most oppositional children is much better accomplished by making them feel capable, big, and rewarded than by making them feel incapable, small, and punished. I resist the notion that you will damage your child psychologically if you say to her in the midst of a meltdown, "You are not allowed to act like this. I want to see some better behavior immediately!" You are much more likely to damage your child psychologically if you do not make her acutely aware of which behaviors are acceptable and which are not. From my perspective, failing to do so is a form of neglect. Defiant behavior, if left unchecked, can ultimately put your child at odds with everyone she will be around on a regular basis.

How Your Child Should Think

When it comes to the issue of how children think, our goal is to help the defiant ones understand that it is their own thoughts and beliefs that often create the tensions they experience with adults. In chapter 2, I talked about the brain game, which I use extensively with exploding children. It turns out that this technique is readily adapted for use with oppositional children from about four and a half years old to around seven.

Remember, the ground rules for the brain game are that I pretend I am part of the child's brain. In using this with defiant children, however, I identify myself as the "arguing part of the brain," the part that always wants to argue with adults but that always gets them in trouble when it becomes the "boss part of the brain." I ask them to be the "in-control part of the brain" in order to keep themselves out of trouble. Because children who are defiant are so sensitive to the issue of who has power, they quickly understand the reasons to remain in control of themselves, and they quickly begin to give appropriate responses. The beauty of this process is that it typically shows you that your child really does know who is who in the family power structure. A brain game session with a six-year-old might sound like this:

ME: Hey, she just made me mad. Let's blow up and tell her she's not the boss of us.

CHILD: No! I'm not going to blow up. Plus, she *is* the boss!

ME: No she's not. Nobody can boss us around.

CHILD: We have to listen to Mom and Dad and do what they say!

ME: No! I don't want anyone telling us what to do!

CHILD: They can tell us what we have to do.

ME: No they can't. Nobody can tell us what we have to do.

CHILD: They can so tell us what to do. If we don't do it, we can get in trouble. We can lose all our stuff if we make them too mad.

ME: I don't care. I want to tell them they're stupid!

CHILD: No! You will get us in too much trouble. I don't want to lose all my stuff.

ME: Are you sure?

CHILD: Yes!

ME: So how should we act?

CHILD: Just do what they tell us to do!

ME: OK, OK, OK, you win! I know you're right.

A final point about playing the brain game with a defiant child is that you always have to end on a positive note. Let her know that you agree, that the in-control part of her brain really does have to be the boss brain. Give her a high-five or a hug for playing it so smartly.

Self-Awareness: What Are You Making Me Think and Feel with Your Behavior?

Another issue that is of supreme importance with defiant children is that they learn how to analyze the impact of their behavior on others. Because of this, I tell parents to use "the question." This is when you look at your child intently (if you wear glasses, look over the top of them for the best effect) and ask, "What are you making me feel like with your behavior right now?"

I have found that with some children, using such a question when you see them ramping up to explode or argue with you can serve as a powerful prompt to get them to regain control of themselves. It makes them aware that their behavior toward you is not impact-free, and neither will it be consequence-free. Do not allow your child to answer "I don't know." You should feel perfectly free to indicate to your child that he is expected to think and learn about his effect on others, and, if necessary, loss of access to toys and treats for a while might give him a good opportunity to do some thinking.

Some young children seem to have a natural awareness of others' feelings, but others have no grasp whatsoever of human emotions. With the latter kids, we have to use procedures to give them a feeling vocabulary. The simplest method is to tell them that the main feelings most people have, aside from just feeling normal, are mad, sad, and glad. If you add worried and afraid to this, you pretty much have a list that will serve most children well in their early socialization. Kids like it when you play a feeling game with them, such as having them guess what feeling you are experiencing by making your face look a certain way. Another technique is to sit with them and watch a video. Pause the video every few minutes and ask, "What is that person making that other person feel with his or her behavior?"

There are several other ways of thinking that you want your child to adopt. I refer to these as rules. You should discuss these rules with defiant children from around the age of eight and up.

Rule one: You must make yourself pleasant to be around. This means knocking it off with the defiant attitude and the explosions when they don't get their way. There will always be some rotten attitude and arguing — they are kids, after all — but it cannot be at a level that dominates family life. I explain to kids that most of the successful people I have known are pretty pleasant individuals to be around, and most of the unsuccessful people I have met are pretty unpleasant individuals to be around. Though admittedly concrete and oversimplified, this viewpoint hooks into their dichotomous thinking style and gives them a clear understanding of how things have to be.

Rule two: You must try your hardest. My favorite story to

tell kids about effort involves two brothers I know. The younger brother, a ninth grader, has marked learning disabilities and really struggles in school. He recently brought his grades up from D's and F's to almost all C's, a monumental improvement. Because of his hard work in this area of his life and others, he is getting more money, freedom, and responsibility.

His brother is another case. Two years older, he is exceptionally bright and charming. He has never had to study and effortlessly gets A's and B's. He puts off all of his schoolwork until the last minute because he can do so with little penalty. It is also quite likely that his teachers give him breaks because of his intellect and personality, and because they want to see him go on to a highly ranked college.

His parents say that he has never pushed himself at anything and avoids activities that he cannot master with little effort. He tried baseball once. He struck out and never played again. I have indicated to him that his super intellect is a happy genetic accident, the result of his internal wiring at conception, but that once he goes to college, he will have to compete with others who are equally smart but who also have developed a strong work ethic. He is not within sniffing distance of the big rewards he says he likes, not even within sight of them, because he does not truly challenge himself.

Rule three: You must hang out with kids who are headed in a positive direction. Many of the defiant kids I work with take their friends from among the slackers, liars, thieves, and bullies whom everyone encounters at some point in school. Many of them are quite capable of success but end up boring a hole in the bottom of their own boats due to the friends they choose.

Rule four: You must represent your family well in public. This goes back to my farm boy roots in North Carolina. I can still hear my grandmother saying, "Don't act the fool!" I knew what she meant. If I did not present myself well in public, the public would come to the conclusion that I had been raised by a family of fools. Such an outcome would have been intolerable.

What to Do When Your Oppositional Child Hits You

That farm I was raised on was a small farm in north-central North Carolina. The community I grew up in, Allensville, is as much a state of mind as an actual place. I have never seen it listed on a map.

My memories are of independent, proud adults who insisted that their children grow up to be productive, inventive, polite individuals. The role of a young child was to play, to listen, to learn, to help on the farm, to become smart, and to be polite and respectful. Attempts on my part, or on the part of my peers, to be coequals with the adults were seen as the silly mutinies that they were—children trying to be independent, without a clue as to what that actually entailed. There were, at the end of the day, no questions about who was in control. I have no recollection, none whatsoever, of children hitting their parents, wrecking classrooms, or telling adults to shut up.

So I wonder how my mother or father might have reacted had I done to one of them what one highly oppositional five-year-old boy did in my office. His mother told him to leave my desk lamp alone. He turned around and smacked her right in the arm. Then he turned back to continue fiddling with the lamp, as if nothing had happened.

How is it that parents who bring their children to my office because they are getting hit by them invariably tell me that they would never have considered hitting their own parents? It makes me wonder what has happened to our culture. The farm people who raised me and my contemporaries in Allensville would find it highly amusing that these parents could in any way be hesitant to provide large consequences for such behavior, or spend so much time trying to use talk and reason and logic to convince their child that hitting isn't nice.

As you might guess, the boy who hit his mother so calmly in my office did everything in his power to ignore her attempts to talk to him. As she told me later, the thing that finally got his attention was to let him get very familiar with the four walls of his room. She made sure that he understood that every time he hit, every time he drew back his hand to hit, and every time he verbally threatened to hit, he would immediately and without further discussion be given a significant amount of time to sit in his room and reflect on his behavior.

His initial response to being removed to his room was to wreck everything in an attempt to show his mother that he would simply up the ante if she tried to punish him. He tossed toys everywhere, pulled the mattress off his bed, emptied his dresser drawers, and tried to kick holes in the wall. He did all of this in a very controlled manner, according to his mother, stopping to take breaks along the way and shouting through the door to inform his mother about what he was doing.

Her response, once he had finished, was to tell him that it was now his responsibility to put everything back where it had been and that until he had done so, all other activities and privileges were canceled. Even though he screamed and cried at the consequences, she let him know that it would do him good to learn how to fold clothes and organize everything in his dresser, and that it would also serve him well in life to know how to make his bed and put his toys back into the bins that she had provided. She also had him clean the scuff marks off the wall where he had kicked it with his tennis shoes. Cleaning up his room was not a quick process and occupied the better part of a weekend. Did doing so somehow miraculously give him a new personality? No, he remained strong willed and edgy throughout the time that I had contact with him. However, he ceased hitting his mother, and he never wrecked his room again.

It is critically important to restate that punishment and negative consequences are rarely appropriate or helpful with children who are blowing up or melting down due to road map issues, unexpected transitions, or other issues. Defiant children are a whole different story, as you have just seen. Their outbursts and blowups are conscious strategies used to get their way. While all children act like this at times, oppositional children do it so frequently and so intensely that it dominates family life and every day becomes a haze of fighting, yelling, screaming, and arguing.

It is always best to lead children out of mistaken behavior rather than to attempt to force them out of it, particularly when they have yet to reach puberty. Leading them allows them to learn. Forcing them just raises their defenses, and the more you try to force, the smarter their defenses become. There are, however, children who will not give you much of a chance to lead them out. The strength of their desire to prove that you have no power over them can at times be equal to the strength of your desire to show them a better way. You should turn to punishment and negative consequences only after you have tried all the positive methods and are sure that they have failed.

When I tell adults during my public appearances how much I like working with oppositional children and adolescents, they are frequently puzzled. How can I like kids who cause so much grief with their behavior? I admit that it is sometimes easier for me to find them likable than for their parents to do so because I don't have to live with them day in and day out. However, I also like to remind parents that oppositional children are frequently bright kids with vigorous personalities and an inborn optimism about becoming successful in the pursuit of their goals.

Our ultimate task is to channel all of this energy toward appropriate goals. Often this means that we have to accept the personality that we are working with, warts and all, and try to teach children how to maintain their independence and stay out of trouble with the authorities at the same time.

In dealing with oppositional children, the most important point to remember is that we will do much better in the long run to concentrate on their strengths and to let them know that we are totally aware of their potential. This does not mean that we have to tolerate their behavior when they are stuck in some misguided stage of rebellion. As odd as it might sound, our long-range strategy with a vigorous, independence-seeking child is to teach him or her how to become truly rebellious. This entails first becoming very good at something—science, art, math, sports, drama, and so on—and second pushing the limits of that field with all their might in order to see how far it can take them in life when others their age are sitting around buzzed out on video games or stuck in that stage where mouthing off to the teacher is cool. If we succeed even a little bit, we will have done well.

5

I'M A WIGGLER AND A DAYDREAMER

*

WHY DO I HAVE a section about attention deficit hyperactivity disorder, commonly known as ADHD, in a book about explosive children? While explosive behavior is not a major indicator of ADHD, children with it can definitely be explosive. You are correct to wonder about ADHD if your child's explosions are coupled with distractibility, impulsivity, short attention span, forgetfulness, difficulty completing tasks, or levels of hyperactivity that exceed what you would expect to see in a young child.

Often, teachers are the first professionals to alert parents to the possibility that their child has ADHD. This is because it is not uncommon for an undiagnosed child to display few behavioral symptoms when interacting with others one on one. Place him in a classroom with twenty other children where he becomes overwhelmed by the sights, sounds, and commotion of the group, and his explosions and outbursts come to the fore.

A comprehensive review of ADHD is outside the scope of this chapter. Instead, I will focus primarily on why children with ADHD explode and how to deal with their explosive behavior. Certain facts about ADHD deserve mention. First, among children ages four to seventeen, ADHD affects something over 4 percent of males versus just under 2 percent of females. For this reason, some people jokingly refer to ADHD as the "Y chromosome disorder." We know that boys are much more likely to be referred for ADHD evaluation by their teachers than girls, even when both sexes display the same symptoms. Second, ADHD appears to be largely genetic in origin, with heritability among identical twins ranging from 60 to 90 percent in various studies. Third, there are different subtypes of ADHD. Kids with "ADHD primarily hyperactive" wiggle and rotate in their chairs, have trouble keeping their feet still, blurt out and interrupt, and talk over others. "ADHD primarily inattentive" is marked by forgetfulness, difficulty completing tasks, difficulty with sustained listening, trouble getting details right, and getting bored easily. In "ADHD combined type," children display high levels of both hyperactive and inattentive symptoms. Finally, some children display mild to moderate symptoms of ADHD, while others display extreme symptoms.

The Misnomer Disorder

Whatever ADHD is, it is poorly named. Not a day goes by without a parent telling me that his or her child cannot have ADHD because he can play video games for hours. I don't particularly like to burst anyone's bubble, but I always respond that ADHD children are almost magnetically drawn to visual activities—computer, video, and hand-held games; movies; Legos, Lincoln Logs, and wooden blocks; and taking things apart and (sometimes) putting them back together.

My years of contact with ADHD children have convinced me that they are primarily visual, kinetic, and hands-on processors. Having to attend to anything presented to them in a verbal format, including parent lectures when you're angry with them, forces them to use their weakest cognitive tool—listening. I suspect, as do many of the parents of the children I work with, that ADHD children can actually concentrate quite well in school when they are assigned to teachers who use lots of visual techniques, such as brightly colored overheads and PowerPoint presentations, movies and filmstrips, hands-on activities, and activities that do not leave them chair-bound. My personal vote on the terminology to use when describing these children would be to get rid of the idea that they have some sort of "disorder." I prefer to concentrate on their strengths rather than their weaknesses and would like to refer to them as "visuo-kinetic processors."

I am aware that simply concentrating on a child's strengths, however, will not make the weaknesses disappear. We might decrease some of their distractibility, off-task behavior, and restless feet and hands by employing more visual and hands-on methods of instruction, but this does not change the fact that significant numbers of these children would still remain in a dazed fog, wiggling away at their desks as if driven by tiny motors, totally unaware of what the teacher is teaching.

It is important to remember that such symptoms are not under the child's control. Children who are inattentive or disruptive or who get up and roam around the classroom can control their behavior for brief periods of time, but they can't simply stop being inattentive or disruptive regardless of the training or the rewards we might offer them. This is because the driving forces behind ADHD behavior do not appear to be motivational or psychological. Rather, they seem to be neurological in origin. A growing body of evidence shows that there are physical differences between an ADHD brain and a non-ADHD brain, such as differences in size of the right hemisphere and differences in the tissues that connect the two hemispheres of the brain.

Meet Phillip

All of the science that has been poured into researching the signs and symptoms and statistics of ADHD is interesting, but it does not show what it is actually like to talk to a child who has it. I'm going to invite you into my therapy room so that you can meet

Phillip, age eight. He has a history of frequent explosions at home. He also has trouble concentrating at school, but he generally creates no problems there except that the kids who sit near him complain about his constant motion. He occasionally gets in trouble for bringing toy soldiers to school and attempting to play with them as his teacher talks. He takes stimulant medication, which seems to help moderate his behavior only partially. When his medication begins to wear off, he becomes very touchy—a common side effect of stimulants. His mother tells me that this is when many of his explosions take place. Phillip was prescribed an extra dose of medication to tide him over until bedtime, but this interfered with his ability to go to sleep at a reasonable hour. Phillip has lost virtually of his privileges due to his forgetfulness, inability to finish tasks and homework, and explosive behavior at home. His mother is at a loss for what to do next and is confused about how accountable she should hold him for his actions.

ME: Hi, Phillip. Do you know why your mom brought you here to talk today?

PHILLIP: No. Is this your office?

ME: Yes, it is my office. You don't have any idea at all?

PHILLIP: Do you live here?

ME: No, I just use this office for talking to kids. Has your mom ever talked to you about your behavior at home or anything like that?

PHILLIP: I don't know.

ME: OK. Well, let me tell you what I know is going on. I understand that your dad is in Korea right now. I bet you miss him.

PHILLIP: Yeah.

ME: Have you been worrying about him a lot?

PHILLIP: No. He told me not to worry. Is that fan up there yours?

ME: Yes, it came with my office. You're not worried about your dad at all?

PHILLIP: No.

ME: Great. I like it when guys aren't worried. So let me tell you why you and your mom are here today. I understand that lately you've been having some pretty big explosions. Your mom says you blow up pretty big sometimes, and our job is to try to figure out why this happens and see what we can do about it.

PHILLIP: What?

ME: I said your mom tells me that you've been having some big explosions and blowups lately, and we have to figure out how to make them stop.

(Phillip looks blank and begins to play with his fingers.)

ME: Did you hear what I said?

PHILLIP: Yes.

ME: What did I say?

PHILLIP: You said my dad was gone.

ME: Do you remember anything I said after that?

PHILLIP: Yes.

ME: What did I say?

(Phillip again looks blank, shrugs his shoulders, and continues playing with his fingers.)

ME: Mister Phillip, please stop playing with those fingers while we talk. It makes it so you can't hear what I'm saying.

PHILLIP: No it doesn't.

ME: What have I been talking to you about so far?

PHILLIP: My fingers?

You can see where this is headed. It is clear that Phillip was so distracted by his own fingers that it was very hard to talk to him. I had hoped to spend the session discussing his explosions, but it readily became evident that such a goal was too lofty, at least for that first day. Instead, I taught Phillip and his mother how to play the "statue game," a technique for helping Phillip learn to monitor what his body is doing. In the statue game, the players compete to see who can sit still, like a statue, the longest. Phillip liked playing the statue game with me in our later sessions and relished the idea that he could sit still longer than I could and could catch me when I made the smallest movement.

For Phillip, stillness is a foreign concept, and like many children with ADHD, he has very little awareness of what his body is doing at any given time. His constant finger play, foot movement, and tendency to stare at the area just to the right of the person he is talking to make it quite difficult for him to hear much of what is being said.

Why Children with ADHD Explode

Children like Phillip explode for myriad reasons. Obviously, they test the patience of others, who often resort to yelling and screaming and demanding, which in turn causes the child to explode. Next, their impulsiveness makes them prone to not think very far into the future in a way that would give them insight into the effect their behavior may have on others. They seem to lack that mental filter that makes you think before you act. If they think it, they do it.

Their explosions also may be due to the important fact that sometimes they suffer from a second and sometimes even a third disorder. For example, children with ADHD frequently also display the symptoms of oppositional defiant disorder. They may also suffer from anxiety, be depressed, or display the symptoms of obsessive-compulsive disorder. All of these conditions are associated with explosive behavior and are covered in more depth elsewhere in this book. It is important that any therapist or physician who works with your child consider these diagnoses as well.

I am of the opinion that the predisposition to engage deeply in visually oriented tasks is another reason that children with ADHD explode. When they get involved in a video game, a Lego project, or even daydreaming, they are in no way unfocused, and no attention deficit is evident. Instead, they are hyperfocused, totally locked in. When a child gets hyperfocused, the rest of the world disappears, and he notices very little of what is going on around him. I have had mothers tell me that they can run the vacuum cleaner right past an ADHD child who is engaged in a video game, and he will hardly notice. This is why Phillip's mother typically had to tell him six times to turn the video game off and come to dinner. In many ways, hyperfocused children are like road map kids. Once they are locked in to an activity, they are loath to give it up.

Another pressure point for ADHD children is homework. I suspect that their ability to focus on verbally oriented subjects such as language arts and social studies is in inverse proportion to their ability to focus on visually oriented tasks. Because of this, they don't want to stop doing what they are doing and go face a pile of books and work sheets. Even when you get them physically to the homework table, there is no guarantee that the work will go peacefully. They will take three hours to do a half-hour's work because they are staring out the window or at the ceiling, or they are constantly getting up to sharpen their pencils. At some point in this process, they get so frustrated by all of the homework they still have to do that they explode. And who can blame them? For many children on stimulant medication, homework time is when the medication is wearing off. Parents must be considerate of the fact that this is beyond the child's control.

When ADHD children explode, you are likely to hear all of their thoughts and doubts about themselves come tumbling out. They often know that they are different from other kids, and this makes them feel bad. They somehow consistently manage to lose both their homework and their lunch on the ride to school. Their teachers are always on their case. The other kids laugh at them when the teacher asks them a question and that deer-in-the-headlights look makes it obvious to everyone that they were off in la-la land.

ADHD kids who are struggling come to secretly think of themselves as dumb or stupid, which also leaves them feeling cranky and unhappy. As I stressed earlier, children often think in terms of dichotomies. A child who is struggling comes to believe that there are only two kinds of kids—smart and dumb. The reason that the child ignores the "average" group in this equation is that when she is struggling, *everyone* seems smarter than she is. It is exceptionally important for you and your child to understand that ADHD has nothing to do with intelligence. In general, there is a strong body of evidence indicating that there is no significant difference in the overall intelligence of children with ADHD and those without it.

When a child with ADHD is in the midst of a meltdown, it is sound advice for parents not to take the explosion personally. The child's impulsive nature and difficulty listening may make it hard to follow this advice, but the calmer you remain, the less likely the child will be to lose control.

Treatment Options

The only way to decrease a child's explosions is to address the underlying cause. This is particularly difficult with ADHD, given its apparent neurological origin. Because there is no known cure for ADHD, your goal is to attempt to manage your child's symptoms by attending to as many of the issues that make him explode. This includes a clearheaded consideration of medication, as well as education and training for both you and your child.

Medication

The differences in the production of the neurotransmitters dopamine and norepinephrine in the brains of children who have ADHD compared to those who do not lands every parent smack in the middle of one of the most contentious issues in pediatric medicine: should children be placed on medication for ADHD? A complete review of this issue is outside the scope of this chapter. It should be noted, however, that the single most efficient way to manage ADHD does appear to be through the use of stimulant medications. The 2003 National Survey of Children's Health found that approximately 4.4 million children ages four to seventeen had been diagnosed with ADHD at some point in their lives. Of these, approximately 2.5 million (56 percent) were taking medication for the disorder.

I do not want to jump on the medication bandwagon, but neither do I want to park it so far out in the parking lot that everyone will forget it is there. Medication can be life altering for some children with ADHD, allowing them to live up to their academic potential because they can finally concentrate, pay attention, and stay out of trouble with their peers and teachers. For some children, the effect is dramatic. For others, the medication provides enough help to make it worthwhile. Still other children find no benefit or are troubled by side effects.

With that said, I am a strong advocate of ruling out other causes of inattention, hyperactivity, or off-task behavior before I assume that it must be ADHD. It is well known that children who are anxious, have obsessive-compulsive disorder, or are depressed can be misdiagnosed as having ADHD. Children with allergies and food sensitivities can also have ADHD-like symptoms. To move too quickly to treatment with medication keeps us stuck thinking about only one possible cause of their behavior and perhaps blinded to a whole world of others. Parents would be wise to rule out other potential causes before they turn to medication.

I find that parents today are more and more concerned and disheartened at being told that their children need medication. While I do not necessarily know this in a research way, I do know it in a seat-of-the-pants way. As someone who sits in a chair across from children and their parents many hours per week, I am struck by just how many parents begin their conversations with me by stating that even if their child does end up with an ADHD diagnosis, they do not want to talk about medication. Instead, they want alternatives to medication. In addition, many parents whose children have already tried medication don't like the side effects. Sometimes stimulants can cause children to appear almost drugged, can cause them to lose their appetite, and can interfere with sleep. And as mentioned earlier, sometimes children can become irritable and explosive when their medication starts to wear off—usually at the end of the school day.

Nonmedication Techniques

Most of the nonmedication techniques that may be useful in managing a child's ADHD have not received the same research attention as stimulants and other medications, or they have not been shown to be effective in large group studies. While you should be very suspicious of wide-sweeping claims of a cure for anything, you should also be aware that the failure of a technique in a large group study does not necessarily mean that it will not work for your child. Psychology as a profession has a long history of using what are called "single-subject" research designs. These are studies of small groups of children in which a child's response to a treatment is compared only to his own behavior prior to the treatment. There is typically a phase in which treatment is withdrawn and then reinstituted to see if its effects are predictable.

I encourage parents to adopt this single-subject viewpoint while trying to find what is useful for their child. One very angry mother I once talked to had met with her son's school about the fact that there was black mold growing on the ceiling tiles and she believed that it was having a negative effect on her son's ability to concentrate. The school totally discounted this possibility, because no other children seemed to be suffering any side effects. Subsequent testing found him to be very allergic to mold.

Training in social skills, as well as attending summer training programs aimed at improving peer relationships, interactions with adults, and academic performance, has also been shown to be useful for children with ADHD. There is evidence that seeking such training when your child is very young may be particularly useful for both you and your child because it starts to lay down skills and strategies early in life.

Edmund Sonuga-Barke and his colleagues at the University of Southampton in England investigated an eight-week series of meetings with the mothers of 78 three-year-olds in their homes. The mothers were trained in how to recognize ADHD-type behaviors, how to use demands for eye contact and other verbal commands to help a child maintain appropriate behaviors, how to use reinforcement and praise to increase the number of appropriate behaviors a child displays, and how to use time-out to disrupt the cycle of negative behaviors. These methods were tested against a general supportive counseling approach in which the mothers were allowed to explore issues of concern to them and to express their feelings about the child but in which no specific training in behavioral techniques was offered. For comparison, a waiting list group received no treatment.

Significant changes were noted in the behavior of children whose mothers received training, with those children maintaining their improvements fifteen weeks after the end of training. (It is possible that they maintained their gains even longer, but no further observations were made.) The mothers who received training also noted a distinct improvement in their own subjective sense of well-being, although this appeared to tail off gradually once contact with the trainers ended. Children and mothers who received more general counseling also reported improvements, but at a much less significant level in comparison to the training group. Those on the waiting list, as might be expected, showed no change. The implications of this important study are that reading about ADHD and seeking training in behavioral strategies from mental health experts early in a child's life can have a clear positive impact on his or her behavior, as well as on the parents' satisfaction.

ADHD EXPLOSIONS IN THE CLASSROOM

There are some commonsense techniques that can be used with ADHD children who explode in the classroom. First, make sure they are seated toward the front of the room and away from sources of visual distraction, such as windows and doorways. Also make sure they are seated away from disruptive peers or children they do not get along with. With young children, it can prove quite potent for the teacher to announce to the class that a child has been successfully listening or behaving and to have him receive a round of applause from his peers. The teacher also can circulate around the class as he or she talks and use techniques such as tapping a child's desk to indicate that the child must refocus. If it is evident to the teacher that the child has difficulty with transitions, the teacher can use a countdown technique in which he or she announces how many more minutes the class has before switching activities.

There is also evidence that techniques referred to as "self-monitoring" can be useful with children who have difficulty maintaining attention and staying on task in the classroom. In one study, children were trained to rate whether or not they were on task every sixty seconds when a tone was sounded. The results showed dramatic increases in on-task behavior. One child, for example, went from being on task 16 percent of the time to being on task almost 73 percent of the time. The disadvantage of this procedure is that it uses an audible tone that signals a child to rate himself, something that may not be feasible in all classrooms. In another study, children were trained in a much less intrusive method. They used the classroom clock to rate whether or not they were on task every five minutes. The results showed that off-task behavior decreased dramatically.

In a similar vein, a monitoring system called the Gordon Attention Training System can be used in the classroom with children who have marked difficulty with off-task or disruptive behavior. A small box with a screen is placed on the child's desk. The teacher has a transmitter that controls the device. As long as the child remains on task, the child earns points from the teacher. These points, shown on the readout on the child's box, can be exchanged later for privileges. If the child goes off task or becomes disruptive, the teacher can subtract points from the child's total using the transmitter.

Of great interest, this system has been shown to be as effective as medication in controlling off-task behavior in the classroom. However, once the device is removed from a child's desk, it appears that the child's off-task behavior returns to its earlier, problematic level. That the system does not have a long-term, lasting impact on the child's tendency to go off task is disappointing—but neither does medication. The good news is that children who use the system appear to benefit greatly while they are in the classroom.

HOMEWORK EXPLOSIONS

Let's briefly address the massive outbursts and three-hour sessions of yelling and screaming to complete a half-hour's worth of homework that so many parents complain of. Use of a prompting device to help children move through their work more quickly can reduce these episodes. Prompting devices such as an audiotape that emits a brief tone every sixty seconds or a small, pager-size device that can be set to beep or vibrate as a prompt to keep a child on task are available commercially. My own unpublished research with a group of children who were in counseling with me and who used an audiotape that signaled them every two minutes to remain on task during their homework has led me to believe that the same improvements seen in school-based experiments can be replicated at home.

As in the school studies noted earlier, the child can use a tracking sheet to rate himself on whether or not he is on task when the tone sounds. In the training phases of the process, you must sit with your child and rate him also so that he can learn what constitutes on-task and off-task behavior. Do not be surprised if your child attempts to defeat the program by complaining that the tracking sheet is too hard to use or that having the tone sound every few minutes is too obnoxious. Tell your child that your goal is to use the prompting device to put an end to homework explosions and that if he is successful at this, you will guarantee that he will be well rewarded for his efforts.

It is also generally accepted that in working with a child with ADHD, a predictable homework schedule and a clear set of routines will benefit the child. As much as possible, consider having your child do her homework at the same time every day. In addition, make your meal schedule as predictable as possible.

There is no reason to believe that every fit-throwing ADHD child will become a fit-throwing ADHD teenager or adult. Some will, but most will not. As children age and mature, they learn more and more ways to deal with their own wiring. Children who stare off at ceiling fans and walls and fiddle with their hands and toes while you are trying to talk to them often become aware, by the time they are in high school, that looking at the teacher is the main way to take in material that they are going to be tested on later. They sometimes grudgingly admit that they have to turn off their instant messengers and cell phones if they want to study, and they move past the stage where they argue that they can watch television or play a video game and study at the same time. Thankfully, many middle schools, high schools, and colleges offer instruction in study skills and test-taking strategies. Young children, however, are often not mature enough to take advantage of such strategies.

The reason that I maintain such optimism about ADHD children is that my own experience in dealing with hundreds of them over the years has shown me that they are often bright and inventive, if distracted. In most cases, I believe that their brightness and inventiveness will win out in the end. The fly in the ointment, however, is the issue of motivation. Some children just don't care whether or not they succeed in school and seem content, at least for a while, with marginal performance. To counteract this tendency, you must convince your child early in life that everything is earned. Assure him that you will give him any help that he needs in overcoming the difficulties that ADHD has imposed on him, but caution him that you will not reward lack of effort. Your child also needs to see you working hard to attain your own goals and pushing yourself to achieve certain accomplishments. It is this mindset, I believe, that is ultimately curative for a child struggling with any chronic problem.

The main point to take away from this chapter is that as a parent, you would be wise to add many techniques and philosophies to your bag of tricks in dealing with an explosive ADHD child. Try them out systematically, and keep only the ones that appear to have the most promise for your child. None will be likely to create a lasting change if used only once or twice. But if you use the most promising techniques frequently and your child responds well, you will have a chance to deliver more praise and rewards than criticism and punishments. This, in turn, may result in your child trying just a little bit harder, and no one can argue with that.

6

I CAN'T CONTROL MYSELF AT SCHOOL

*

IT IS STRESSFUL ENOUGH when children explode at home or in the car, but such behavior in the preschool, kindergarten, or elementary school setting adds an extra layer of stress that no parent needs. First, parents are continually threatened with the task of finding a new daycare or preschool, having been told repeatedly, "If he continues to act this way, we just can't keep him." If he is in public school, at some point the issue gets raised of placing him in special education, perhaps even in a self-contained classroom for children who are "emotionally disabled."

Second, the parent's boss might understand at first when he or she has to leave work to go to school to get the child because he hit someone. But the fifth time or the tenth time? An employer's patience can easily run thin.

I ask parents to accept the fact that dealing with a child who explodes at school will never be convenient. There is no magic solution, and it is not the sole responsibility of the daycare center or school to deal with a child who is prone to get out of control. You cannot wash your hands of your child's behavior simply because she is at school. You must be fully engaged in a partnership with school personnel in order to forge a solution, and this means going to meetings and arranging to be on-site as necessary.

The Feedback Loop

If your child is explosive at school, you should request that his teacher supply you with daily feedback on his behavior. While it may seem excessive to give you feedback on your child's behavior on a daily basis, it is the only technique that will make it possible to implement a behavior modification program that ties access to his home reinforcers to his school behavior – something I believe in strongly. Once-weekly feedback on Friday afternoon, for example, gives you no way of dealing with what your child did on Tuesday.

Your child should very definitely be kept in the loop. Tell her that her teacher will be sending ratings of her behavior home on a daily basis and that you and she will sit down and review her teacher's notes. Tell her that not only will you write a response to her teacher about her behavior and how things will be handled at home, but also that she too will have to write a response to her teacher indicating how she intends to correct any problem that was noted that day. (If your child is too young to write, write a response for her after discussing the problem, and have her sign it.)

When teachers give written feedback, it is also extremely important for them to take the time to let children know what they did well rather than centering only on their mistakes. Doing so gives them hope and guidance on how to proceed, while focusing solely on the negative tells them only that they blew it and leaves them stewing in those unproductive juices.

Be ready to deal with your child's resistance to swapping notes back and forth with the teacher. His main strategy may be to insist that his teacher was lying about his behavior. Explain that if he had a great day at school (and a great afternoon and evening at home), life will be good. A bad day at school will reduce his access to his favorite treats and activities. Likewise, a day in which he did well at school but whacks you with all sorts of bad attitude at home will result in a relatively Spartan lifestyle.

What the School Should Do

In addition to using feedback and making a child's access to her favorite activities and treats contingent on her behavior at school, I suggest several other options to counselors and teachers who interact with explosive children on a daily basis.

School counselors, social workers, and psychologists should familiarize themselves with the numerous causes of childhood explosions. It is important for individuals in such positions to avoid becoming attached solely to the belief that Dr. A or Dr. Z (or even Dr. R!) has developed a theory that explains all school explosions and has designed a universal treatment that will make all explosions go away. It is much better to read broadly in the various topics touched on in this book and to develop a well-rounded view of what might be going on with a particular child. We should foster the belief that it is important to treat the underlying causes of the negative behavior, not just the behavior itself.

In addition, it is doubtful that your child is the only exploding child at his school. Perhaps the school counselor could form a group for these children. In group therapy, children set goals for themselves to decrease the frequency and intensity of their school meltdowns, then report their progress back to the group. They also discuss the types of situations that seem to trigger their meltdowns and discuss alternative ways to handle these situations. The school counselor can teach the group members to use techniques such as the brain game, discussed in chapter 2. Older kids may be taught a variety of cognitive and behavioral strategies to use when anxiety about unexpected transitions or road map issues begins to rise.

An important part of your child's contact with the school counselor, whether it is done in a group setting or an individual setting, is the role-playing and exposure that I discussed in chapter 2.

This can be particularly powerful in a group setting. For example, children could be asked to do a simulation of a situation in which one child bumps into another while they are standing in line. The child who gets bumped will have the task of thinking out loud how to handle the situation, with the other group members adding suggestions or praise for good ideas. Group praise for successfully getting through the simulation can be a powerful reinforcer for trying new behaviors. Likewise, simulations can be used to have kids practice getting through unexpected transitions, such as "Put your drawings away; it is now time to begin math," or unexpected events, such as being told in the cafeteria, "Sorry, the pizza is gone. All we have left is tuna salad."

The school counselor, social worker, or psychologist also can serve as a trainer for teachers. Most teachers are already overburdened with instructional tasks and have little time to delve into the theoretical reasons for explosive behavior. The school counselor can hold an in-service workshop to train teachers how to recognize and deal with children who are prone to display explosive behavior, in how to make a referral back to the counselor for group or individual counseling, and in how to have a classroom discussion and do a whole-class exercise on dealing with unexpected events.

Teachers and school counselors can adopt a wide range of strategies that may be useful in getting young children to begin to think about their behavior. For instance, they can use the "big" descriptors that I introduced in chapter 2. A teacher might pull a child aside when she is behaving positively and say, "I really like the way you are acting today; you are acting like a big girl," "You're in the big girl zone today with your behavior," or "I really would like to see more big girl behavior, please." These interactions need not occur within earshot of any other child, and best of all, they can be completed in ten seconds. It may also be powerfully useful for the teacher to announce to the class, "Benjamin has been in the big guy zone all morning with his behavior. Let's give him a round of applause." A round of applause from the class is a potent reinforcer for a young child, something that he is likely to come home bragging about.

Likewise, teachers who send notes home in a child's agenda can tell the parents whether or not their child has acted like a big kid that day. It is important to have all parties use a common set of terms with a young child so that the child does not get confused by the feedback. If the term "big guy" is used at home, the child will be more likely to pay attention when his teacher uses the same language for feedback at school.

The school might consider adopting other, more overarching strategies. There is an interesting body of literature on school attachment and affiliative orientation (the desire to develop and maintain strong relationships with others) indicating that aggression in the school setting can be lowered when schools help children feel deeply engaged with others and with the school itself. Such strategies include consistently rewarding children for self-control and good classroom behavior, rewarding children for being appropriate role models for others, teaching children appropriate assertiveness and coping strategies, and increasing the number of extracurricular activities available to children.

The most effective prevention programs appear to target specific at-risk groups (such as aggressive children) with very specific interventions and to provide more universal, preventive programming, typically employing community, school, and family components. An offshoot of this is that school counselors should run groups for children with identified potential for violent or aggressive behavior and that the parents of these children should be involved in the change process. Family involvement can be done through programs at the school, special programs at community mental health clinics, or programs offered through other agencies.

Schools also must directly address the peer culture operating in their hallways in order to improve the learning environment.

We know that students as young as kindergarten age who get picked on or are rejected by their peers show a decrease in classroom participation and an increase in school avoidance. Combine this with research showing that the younger students are, the more at risk they are for psychological problems, and it becomes apparent that providing a healthy stage for our "littlest learners" is of the utmost importance.

Finally, schools can take a functional look at the classroom environment to determine what forces might keep a child from acting out. Training children not to pay attention to their classmates who are acting out can result in a decrease in disruptive behavior. In addition, providing afterschool programs may result in improved classroom behavior. It has been shown that low-income children who participate in afterschool programs exhibit improved classroom behavior, as well as improved peer relationships and emotional adjustment.

Parent On-Site

I want to return to what individual parents can do in cooperation with the school to bring a halt to a child's outbursts at school. It is absolutely necessary for you to engage in talk and appropriate consequences when your child blows up at school. However, talking to him at home, several hours after an incident at school has occurred, is less than optimal. As I suggested earlier, you should go over the teacher's report with your child, discuss what he should have done, and have him write a letter to his teacher telling her how he will do better.

Suppose, however, that this gets you nowhere. A procedure that can be used to intensify the process for preschoolers and kindergartners (and can also be used with older children if only as a threat — it is guaranteed to get their attention) is for one parent to arrange to be at the school for lengthy periods of time — an entire morning or an entire afternoon, for example — to intervene directly at the time of an incident. Talk to your child's teacher to find out what time of day a blowup or meltdown is most likely to occur and be on-site at that time. Not every parent's work situation will allow this, but those who can manage it say that it works well.

Some schools will allow parents to sit quietly in the hallway, outside the child's classroom. Other parents use a variation on this strategy. They sit in the school parking lot doing paperwork or reading, cell phone at the ready, so that the child's teacher can alert them about an impending meltdown and they can hustle into the classroom. One parent told me that simply appearing out of nowhere and surprising her child in the midst of a meltdown gave him such a shocking experience that he never did it again.

Once you are alerted that your child is melting down, you can quietly enter the classroom, take your child by the hand, and lead him out into the hallway. At this point, you have several options. If your child quiets down quickly and regains his self-control, you can speak to him for a few minutes in the hallway, making him aware that his classroom behavior was not in the big kid zone and you expect more. If necessary, you can also warn him that, sadly, he has just reduced his privileges for the evening. One more outburst will guarantee that he will lose all of his privileges.

It is important to discuss with him how he should have acted, something parents frequently forget to do. We are sometimes quick to tell a child that his current behavior is inappropriate, somehow assuming that he will figure out what the alternatives should be. This might work for some children some of the time, but when a young child is caught up in his own outburst, it is hard for him to see the alternatives. Unless we give him suggestions for how he should have acted instead—suggestions that I refer to as "replacement behaviors"—he will be left knowing only that what he did was wrong, without a clue as to what to do instead.

Before you take him back into the classroom, tell him that he will have to apologize to his teacher for his behavior, because big guys admit their mistakes and work hard to fix them. Let him know that he will have to tell his teacher that he will do better next time. Also tell him that if he works hard at making changes, he will be rewarded with lots of fun.

If your child is out of control when you take him out of the classroom — kicking, screaming, hitting — instead of trying to talk to him in the hallway, where he is likely to remain disruptive, arrange to take him to the principal's or school counselor's office for a talk. If he is still out of control there, take him home. Most likely, your child will have calmed down by the time you get home, which will allow you to have a brief discussion about what he did to get himself in trouble and how he should have acted instead. If you live close to the school, take him back and have him apologize to the teacher for his disruptive behavior. If it is not reasonable to return to school, make sure that he does not inadvertently end up being rewarded by having access to snacks, treats, toys, or video games. Instead, deny him access to these things for the rest of the day.

A twist on this particular program for the truly oppositional six- to ten-year-old who remains stubbornly resistant to change is to inform her that since you had to take time off from work to be at school because of her behavior, you are losing money by not working. Given this loss of income, the child will have to pay you back for coming to school. Since the child does not have any money, the only way she can repay you is in kind. This means that the child will spend the evening doing chores and jobs. Although some parents might think this is too tough, others see it as simple common sense, a way of letting the child know that all behaviors have consequences and that she will be held directly responsible for her behavior.

Keep in mind that you should not use this technique unless you are absolutely certain that your child's behavior was due to purposeful, oppositional behavior. Also, you should not move to this intensified form unless you find that talk-oriented procedures are not working with your child. If you attempt to use this payback procedure and it makes the situation even worse, drop it like a hot rock. Some children respond well to such techniques, but others simply find it to be too much. As with all techniques, you must find the appropriate balance. Children will not respond to interventions that are not intense enough, but neither will they learn from ones that are too intense.

Keep in mind that you should always be looking for the silver lining. If you go to school in the morning, for example, and your child does not melt down, ask the teacher's permission to take him out into the hallway briefly to hug and praise him for his big kid behavior. If the timing is right, you might wish to join him for lunch as a reward for his success, or if it's at the end of the day, drive him home from school and stop somewhere for a big kid treat. That night at dinner, announce to your family that he had a big kid day, then have the family deliver a round of applause and congratulations for his behavior. Children love this type of feedback and take it seriously.

A Warning About Warnings

If I mentally sort through my clinical work with young children from before the mid- to late 1990s, I find almost no cases of children hitting and kicking their teachers or parents. There were clearly cases of children who were hard to control in the classroom, and there were many children who could be aggressive toward their peers, although aggression on the part of the youngsters a decade or more ago came mainly in the form of one child snatching a toy away from another. Being willing to attack adults is a relatively new phenomenon that has appeared during a time when we are trying to use communication and warnings more, not less. I find this particularly troubling.

A whole industry revolves around this notion of giving children warnings about their behavior at school. In the area where I live, preschool and kindergarten classrooms employ color schemes such as red/yellow/green, or even more elaborate ones such as green/orange/red/blue/purple, to warn students about their behavior. Each child has a card, and if his behavior begins to degrade, the teacher moves the card from green, for example, to the next color "down" (green representing the best behavior). As the card gets moved successively lower, the teacher might send the child's parents a note, or the parents may end up having a conference with the principal.

I worry about giving too many warnings. First, if we warn children frequently but provide no real consequences, we are literally teaching them that it is safe to ignore us. This tells those who are prone to act out that their negative behavior has no real consequences.

Some people may find it objectionable when I say that parents must cross their child's threshold of attention with their consequences, or misinterpret it to mean that I am an advocate of harsh punishment. I am, in fact, an advocate of using only enough consequences to get a child's attention. For example, you would probably howl if I seriously suggested to you that if your child brought her grades up from C's and D's to A's and B's, you should reward her with a bowl of broccoli. This reward would have no value to the child, and there is little chance that she would feel rewarded. Likewise, if your child is repeatedly explosive in the classroom and hits or kicks the teacher, you are probably not going to get his attention by giving him a five-minute time-out and telling him not to do it again. The consequences we deliver must be strong enough to get a child's attention, whether we are talking about a reward or a punishment. Without sufficient intensity, we stand little chance of modifying a child's behavior. This again points out the importance of linkages between home and school, which help create that sense of intensity.

Second, if I warn a child repeatedly about her behavior, I am teaching her that she does not have to learn to anticipate consequences — I will do it for her. She will begin to use me as her brain instead of learning to anticipate what will happen for herself.

Some of the parents I work with whose children do not respond to warnings at home have had positive outcomes by moving to a no warning system. The next time your three-, four-, or five-year-old attempts to hit you, do not make any comment at all. Simply pick him up, hustle him off to his room, and do whatever is necessary to enforce a lengthy time-out, followed by a substantial loss of privileges after the time-out. Do not be particularly worried if he is yelling, "What'd I do? What'd I do?" Use it as an experiment to see if the frequency of the hitting goes down when you respond immediately, decisively, and without warning.

I can anticipate the objections that some people might have to this technique. However, I want you to think about it as being what behavioral psychologists refer to as a "shaping procedure." Our behavior gets shaped by what happens after we do a behavior. In a class full of boys, if one boy burps and someone laughs, you can bet he's going to do it again pretty soon. It can work the other way, too. If you begin to think in such terms, you will understand why it works so well to give a child who ignores warnings at home or at school zero reinforcement for his behavior.

Why Mikey Explodes

It's time to let you play detective, to see if you can figure out why a particular four-year-old exploded so violently at his preschool. Here are the observable events. On some days, Mikey was placed at the back of the line, where he had to walk several steps behind the other kids in the company of his teacher's assistant, because he cannot keep his hands to himself. On other days, he was allowed to walk at the front of the line with his teacher, at which point he had to stay several steps in front of the other kids so that he could not easily turn and mess with anyone. At still other times, he had to walk toward the middle of the line, but several steps to the left or the right, walking parallel to his peers so that he could not grab them or poke them. On the day in question, Mikey was in the back when one of his classmates, a girl, moved out of the line. When she came back to the line, she stepped to the rear, not wanting anyone to think that she was cutting back into the line. This meant that she was now behind Mikey. Mikey turned and blasted her, right on the forehead.

Mikey is in clear danger of being kicked out of his private school. Though known to be generous and tolerant in its viewpoint about the nature of children, the school cannot knowingly expose its students to a child who hurts others. I should mention that this was Mikey's third such incident in three weeks, and the school now has him pegged as being dangerous, a powder keg of a child who has proven repeatedly that he will go off with no evident provocation.

Does Mikey really explode for no reason? The answer, of course, is no. Children do not explode for no reason. There is always something going on with them when they do.

When Mikey's mother arrived at the school to pick him up, he told her that he blew up and hit the girl because she "broke in line behind me." I must admit that this was a new one for me. Having occupied the psychologist's chair for many years by the time I met Mikey, I had never before heard of a child blowing up because someone got in line behind him.

I also must admit that at first I didn't get it. Looking back on the incident now makes me even more aware of the fact that when I don't understand why a child does something, I need to take my own advice and listen more closely and ask more questions. When I spoke with the principal on the phone, I began to get it. Mikey had told her that earlier in the day his teacher had promised that when the kids got in line for the water fountain after their play period, he could be the "caboose."

I then called his mother to ask whether she knew about this, and she said that she did but had forgotten to mention it to me. She also said that Mikey had told her that he wanted to be the caboose because when no one else stood behind him in line, he would not feel rushed at the water fountain. He hated it when he couldn't take his time to drink his fill without other kids squawking at him to hurry up and finish so that they could drink, too. Mikey had told his mom this but had not told his principal. There were pieces of the puzzle lying all over the place. Once put together, they would help us understand why he exploded that day.

Knowing these details made it possible to begin to look at the situation through Mikey's eyes and to determine that his explosion was a road map meltdown. Mikey had it firmly in his head that he would be last in line and that no one could get in line behind him, thereby messing up his plan to peacefully drink his fill.

When we met to talk about this incident, Mikey told me that he had been waiting for his chance to drink his fill all morning. His past behavior tells us that he has the type of temperament that leaves him prone to elevate his wants and desires to impending reality, believing them to be something that is absolutely bound to happen. He has never handled surprises or unexpected transitions well. He gets cranky if he thinks he is riding with his mother to the grocery store and she stops at the dry cleaner first. God help his family if he is watching his favorite cartoon and the power goes off. He can rage for hours over something like that.

Mikey's emotional stability depends entirely on his predictions coming true. Knowing that this was a road map issue allowed us to use very exact interventions in an attempt to help him learn to get through such events without blowing up. For example, his parents became vigorous at exposing him to surprises and unexpected events, as discussed in chapter 2. They would tell him they were headed to the grocery store but stop at the hardware store first. They would change their minds about which restaurant to eat at. They would change the routes they took to most of the places he was used to going to, something that he was keenly aware of and sensitive to.

They also went to his school after everyone had gone home and had him role-play remaining calm when he was interrupted at the water fountain or when someone bumped into him or cut

Statements from Parents Regarding School-Related Meltdowns

As in other chapters, it is interesting to hear from parents who have used some of the methods that I've covered in this chapter.

I saw the first child, H., who was six, briefly because of his outbursts at school and his inability to accept unexpected changes and transitions. I taught him all about big kid behavior and about why changes and surprises made him blow up. His mother wrote:

> When we came to see you, I was at my wits' end. I was receiving reports of tantrums during the day at his school. He was frequently frustrated when various things did not go his way. When these occurred, it was nearly impossible to calm him down. They had to "run their course" before he would calm down again.
>
> The big kid/little kid feedback on his behavior has been one of the biggest helps. Whenever he would begin to throw fits or begin to whine or cry, using these terms helped him and us to understand how he should act. Exposing him to unexpected surprises helped him to get used to changes in his day. The more we practiced this, the fewer tantrums we had.

S., who was about to enter kindergarten, had similar success in learning to cope with his need to be in control. His mother wrote:

> He has always been a child who likes structure and doing the same thing at the same time and in the same way each day. He constantly wants me to tell him what time it is, even if there is a clock in plain sight. He also likes to know exactly where we are going whenever we get in the car.
>
> At preschool, he would argue with his teacher if he was asked to do his morning work in a different order or to go to another classroom for testing. Once, when the teacher tried to force him to comply with a change, he exploded, becoming physically aggressive with her and other students. When

the teacher tried to restrain him, he scratched her and tried to bite her. He would also get upset and frustrated if he was unable to complete a task or assignment correctly the first time. He would often ball up his paper and refuse to complete the work when this happened.

This summer, we have been shuffling his schedule quite a bit. Mealtimes vary each day and we often do evening activities in the morning or vice versa. When we go to a familiar place, I often vary the route. When I tell him our agenda for the day's errand, I'll throw in an extra stop or two, or omit something that was on the original plan. At first, he did not like the changes, but he is now learning to go with the flow.

---

in line. Doing this at the site where the troublesome behavior takes place is much more effective than simply talking about it in the abstract or doing role plays at home.

Mikey provided me with a lesson that I needed to work on, even at this late stage of my career. His story keeps me keenly aware that when a child explodes at school, particularly when the explosion includes hitting, everyone will be prone to diagnose him as having oppositional defiant disorder or being a violent child. But there are many other causes of outbursts that are simmering just below the surface, and if we keep observing children and allowing them to tell us their stories, these hidden causes will often make themselves known. Had I not listened to Mikey or simply come to the conclusion that he exploded because he was a brat or a bad kid, I would have failed him miserably.

7

I WORRY ABOUT EVERYTHING

THERE ARE SOME explosive kids who blow up because they worry too much. Some of them are perfectionists, for example, always trying to do everything without error. They explode because their ability to remain calm is so tightly linked to their attempts to be perfect that even the smallest mistake leaves them wild with rage. These are the kids who smack themselves and rip up their homework after they have erased a hole in it because they were trying to get one particular letter to look just right. Or the ones who throw fits on the baseball field after striking out or making an error. They fling helmets and bats and kick water coolers in imitation of their major-league counterparts.

Other worriers have safety issues. They obsess about getting killed or being taken away in the middle of the night by bad men or ghosts or monsters. These children often hide their symptoms well. They leave their parents scratching their heads and wondering why their kids won't sleep in their own beds, won't stay all night at a friend's birthday sleepover, insist that everybody has to come to their house to play, or run shrieking in terror when a parent disappears from their sight. They do not explode in the same manner as the perfectionists. Rather, safety-obsessed, separation-anxious children are apt to act in a markedly frantic way, at times displaying the kind of fear you might see from someone being stalked in a horror movie.

The Prevalence of Anxiety Disorders in Children

The website of the U.S. Department of Health and Human Services' National Mental Health Information Center (mentalhealth.samhsa.gov) provides an excellent description of childhood anxiety disorders. It lists them by type.

Generalized anxiety disorder — children who have unrealistic worries about most everyday activities

Separation anxiety disorder — children who have marked difficulty being away from their parents

Phobias — fears of specific events or objects

Panic attacks — periods of intense fear without any objective cause

Obsessive-compulsive disorder, well known to the public as OCD — includes behaviors such as irresistible urges to wash your hands or an unexplained need to keep things in perfect order

Post-traumatic stress disorder — typically caused by experiencing a hugely stressful event and later having flashbacks, troublesome thoughts about the event, and a greatly decreased sense of safety

The site indicates that about thirteen of every one hundred children and adolescents between the ages of nine and seventeen experience an anxiety disorder of some type. Girls are more prone to experience these disorders than boys, and about half of the children and adolescents diagnosed with an anxiety disorder have a second, comorbid disorder.

It is known to be difficult to diagnose anxiety in very young children, those under the age of six. However, Susan Warren and her colleagues in the psychiatry department at George Washington University have shown that it is possible to use a modified version of the criteria traditionally used to diagnose older children and adults to identify children between the ages of eighteen months and five years who are displaying symptoms of social phobia (difficulty approaching and interacting with others, for example) and generalized anxiety disorder. The obvious importance of this is that early identification of these children can lead to early intervention, hopefully taking them off the road toward depression and anxiety that they may otherwise travel as they age.

We know that anxiety is linked to various genetic factors. A study conducted in the United Kingdom looked at more than four thousand sets of four-year-old twins in an attempt to examine these factors. It found particularly strong genetic links for obsessive-compulsive behaviors and shyness/inhibition. It also found that while a child may be born with a tendency to respond sharply to separation from his parents, his ultimate response is also influenced by his interactions with others in his environment.

Little is known about why children actually develop anxiety disorders. We all know that anxiety itself is a normal part of life for children, as seen in their hesitancy to be around strangers, their difficulty separating from their parents, and their anxiety about novel situations. Anxiety that reaches the level of a disorder can reasonably be thought of as normal worries multiplied by ten, although such a description does not tell us why some children's anxiety stays within the normal range and others' does not.

Inside the Mind of a Worried Child

There are a number of things we should understand about worried children. Like Nostradamus, the famous Renaissance seer, they are always trying to predict what will happen in the future. And like him, they are always predicting apocalyptic events.

The difference is that they are not predicting disasters of the cultural type. They are predicting disasters of the personal type: "I am bound to stink at this," or "I am bound to fail at that." They worry about mistakes that they haven't made yet—borrowing trouble from the future. They worry about their worrying and will tell you that they know the way they think is not the way other kids think. They know they would feel better if they could just give up the worrying, but giving it up is not easy. It is, after all, the way they have always thought. Being anxious, they are as loath to try new ways of thinking as they are to try new foods, new games, or new places.

How else can you recognize the worriers? If you see your child in the following list of behaviors, it is possible that he or she is a worrier.

- Boy worriers often develop a reputation with other boys as being rigid and anxious. Their lack of looseness prevents them from learning to take a joke, and if they get bumped into or whacked while playing sports, they act as if the other child was trying to hurt them on purpose. They often avoid activities that bring them into vigorous physical contact with others. Because of this, they ultimately get rejected by other boys and often develop friendships with girls instead. While the concept of their being friends with girls might warm the hearts of some moms in the audience, it makes most dads cringe. We know what happens to boys who do not fit in with the guys. They become marginalized and rejected by their male peers. While they might develop special talents and become successful once they are out of high school, they carry the scars of their rejection for years to come in the form of self-doubt and resentment toward more physical males.

- Worriers who are perfectionists are rule-bound. They often try to tell other kids what they should be doing and get upset when everyone does not follow the rules in a lockstep manner. One child I knew tried to tell all of her riding partners—adults included—where to sit at the restaurant they always went to after they left the stable. Her inflexibility made her seem controlling and not much fun to be around.

- Worriers are so tense that other kids know that they can easily set them off by calling them names or teasing them. In this regard, they provide great entertainment for their less worried peers.
- Because they spend most of their mental energy on their worries, they often fail to develop social skills and don't learn how to interact with their peers in a fluid, easygoing manner. They never think to ask other children what they like to do or what they are interested in. This makes them appear self-centered and closed to the opinions of others.
- They ask too many questions about normal activities that other kids engage in without undue concern. This alerts you to the fact that they are desperately trying to figure out whether they will get hurt. "Has anyone ever fallen off those monkey bars? How hard is the ground under them? Do you think there could be broken glass on the ground under those monkey bars?"
- They make excuses. "I can't climb the rope in gym class today because I hurt my hands last night. I might hurt my hands even worse if I try." Or, "I can't ride the roller coaster today. I have a cold, and all the wind from going fast might make me sicker."
- Over time, their lives can get more and more constrained if their fears begin to dominate them. They used to walk around the neighborhood without trouble. Now they want to play only in their own backyard.
- They overreact to illnesses or injuries, believing that their prophecy of a horrible end for themselves is about to be fulfilled.

While all of these worries are capable of dominating a child's life and shredding any potential for happiness, the level of worrying that goes with OCD multiplies this by several orders of magnitude. For example, some children with OCD develop secret habits and rituals that make them feel safe and believe that it is absolutely necessary for them to follow through on their habits and rituals. Some germ-phobic kids wash their hands twenty times a day, for example, or take five showers. If unable to follow through on these drives, they do not feel safe or comfortable.

One girl I know has to end each sentence with a particular upward lilt to her voice. If she fails to do so, she has to say the sentence over again.

Another boy has to enter every doorway by stepping through it with his right foot. He will do a little dancelike shuffle as he approaches the doorway in order to adjust his timing to allow him to step through it as he believes he must. Finally, another little girl refused to sit on the carpeted floor at school during story time because she was convinced there "might" be a sharp staple or pin that could stick her and give her deadly germs.

Treatment Options

While I am not of the belief that you should turn to medication simply because a child is anxious, worried, or explosive, there is ample evidence to indicate that medication can be quite useful in bringing a halt to the worrying and obsessions that rob an OCD child of childhood. Between 40 and 60 percent of individuals diagnosed with OCD get at least partial relief by taking a selective serotonin reuptake inhibitor (SSRI). It is also important to note that response rates for exposure-based therapies and cognitive therapies are similar to those for medication, so there is more than one option for the treatment of OCD.

If your child displays the obsessive, ritualistic behaviors seen in OCD (excessive hand washing, having to line up objects or keep them in a certain order, excessive need to clean, and so on), in my opinion it is crucial to consult with his physician to get a referral to both a child psychiatrist who can determine whether medication is advised and a therapist skilled in the various psychological approaches to OCD. With that said, in the remainder of this chapter, I will limit my suggestions to treating the anxious, worried exploders and not the children who suffer from full-blown OCD.

You might be tempted to use the exposure-based therapy techniques I described in chapter 2 with your worried child, and in many cases they will work. Take perfectionistic children, for example. In my book *The Depressed Child,* I described how to desensitize children to their mistakes by giving them mistake homework. I use this technique with many children who believe that their mistakes are horrible events, who blow up and weep as if a catastrophe has occurred when they spill their juice or can't get a drawing to look perfect.

I ask one of the child's parents to role-play making a mistake, using a technique similar to the role-play procedures I described in chapter 2. In this scenario, the parent pretends to be the "child." The real child watches the "child" engage in some activity that she is perfectionistic about, such as signing her name on a piece of paper. The "child" begins to grow obviously more agitated as he or she is unable to do it perfectly. The "child" mutters out loud about how horrible it is, moans and groans, and ultimately rips up the paper and falls on the floor in a fit. By this point, most real children will be having a great time watching the "child" act in such an outrageous manner.

After this, the "child" goes through the act of signing his or her name, saying that he or she doesn't have to get it perfect and that it is important to stay calm.

Following this, the real child is asked to role-play the same scenario. She is asked to pretend to get so frustrated that she melts down completely, yelling, screaming, and rolling on the floor—whatever will help illustrate to her the absurdity of throwing a fit over such an unimportant issue. As above, the real child then does a role play in which she struggles to write her name but resists the urge to erase continually in an attempt to make the letters perfect. During this time, she also prompts herself to remain calm by saying aloud, "I'm in control," "I'm going to stay calm," or something similar.

Following this role play, the child is tasked with making several mistakes a day. Engaging in mistake training with your child is a prime way for you to keep things lighthearted, so that your child learns not to worry about everyday mistakes. For example, I once worked with a child who would melt down horribly if he got anything on his shirt or pants. I gave the father and son the task of putting on old shirts and going to a fast-food restaurant. I told them to get burgers and to be sure to add lots of ketchup to them. They were then to eat their burgers in a way that guaranteed they would get ketchup on their shirts. The boy's job was to remind himself that this was no big deal, that he could put his shirt in the washer when he got home. His father told me later that they had a riot doing this, that it helped his son ease up about his mistakes, and that it had the added benefit of pulling them closer together.

If you decide to use mistake training with your child, tell him that he has to adopt a certain set of thoughts as his own: Mistakes are no big deal. Almost every mistake that a kid makes can be fixed easily. You have to take responsibility for your mistakes and fix them. Your mistakes mean nothing negative about you unless you continue to make the same mistake over and over—at which point you have to admit that you are failing to learn from your mistakes and you have to ask yourself why.

During mistake training, you will be observing how the child acts when he makes a real mistake. If you see him remain calm, you know that the mistake practice is having a positive effect. If he continues to blow up, obviously more work is needed to desensitize him to his mistakes. It is likely that the professional help of a child psychiatrist, a child psychologist, a clinical social worker, or a professional counselor who is trained in such issues is in order.

You can also use exposure therapy with children who panic and overreact because they are afraid to be away from you in your house. I once worked with a young child who was afraid to go into certain rooms in his house alone (particularly upstairs rooms) for fear that something bad would happen to him. He would flip out and explode if he lost sight of his parents. We solved this handily by teaching him how to use a stopwatch. His initial task was to go into various rooms alone and time himself in each room for one minute. He was not allowed to go into the same room repeatedly. He could then trade the minute for a token, which he could in turn trade for special activities, toys, or treats. As he got better at it, we increased the amount of time that he would have to stay in a room to earn a token. We also made the tokens more valuable so that he would not feel as if he was getting ripped off. He soon lost his fears and stopped pitching fits and tantrums and having explosions when it was necessary to go into any of the rooms alone.

The Issue of Proof

Sometimes the source of a child's fears is an elusive target. What do you do when your child's fear is death, being kidnapped, or being harmed by bad people? Certainly, we do not want to expose a child to such situations in any meaningful way. This is where we turn to the cognitive side of cognitive behavior therapy.

All fears are based on proof. Some people are anxious because they have been harmed or been made fearful by some real event in their lives. This provides them with proof that the world is dangerous and they must maintain a constant vigil. For most worried kids, however, proof lies simply in the fact that they believe that something bad *might* happen. In either case, if you want to solve the issue of deep safety anxiety with a child in the six- to ten-year-old range, you have to help her see that she actually has no real proof that something bad is bound to happen. There are a number of ways to do this, some of which children find quite fun.

It might strike you as odd that I would describe working with children's anxieties as "fun." My point is for you to understand that if you take a child's anxieties too seriously, it will possibly appear that you are afraid of the same thing the child is afraid of, which itself is proof that the child is truly doomed. When a child sees you acting in a lighthearted manner, it sends a message that he or she can feel safe because you feel safe.

I want to tell you about "meteorite therapy," something I do with children who worry about everything. After I listen for a while and it is clear that they are overdoing it with the worrying, I ask everyone in the room—typically the child, the parents, and myself—to put one of my big textbooks on their heads (might as well use them for something other than taking up space!). The kids typically look puzzled, as do the parents. Once we are all sitting there with textbooks on our heads, I explain that there are, as we speak, meteorites hurtling through space and that these will break up into smaller chunks as they enter our atmosphere. I then explain that these chunks will fall through the sky and that it is possible that one of the chunks could come through the roof of my office and whack one of us on the head.

Typically at this point, the child is laughing and is thinking that perhaps I am worrying too much. I say to the child, "But it *could* happen. It's not *impossible!*" I find that the more I argue in a lighthearted, humorous manner that a meteorite might whack me on the head at any moment, the more children insist that I am being silly or stupid. This is exactly my point. I want them to see that I am overworrying about something that is not likely to happen, just as they are. I want them to leave my office lightened up, if only for a few minutes, just so they can experience the alternative to their worried mood.

I also want to tell you about what I call "probability therapy." I often use this with kids who pitch massive fits about sleeping alone in their own bedrooms—one of the most common issues with anxious children between the ages of five and eight or so. Invariably, they are afraid of monsters/ghosts/spookies/bad guys, believing that they will be captured or harmed if they stay in their rooms alone. Once I understand that this is a child's issue, I go out to my front office and borrow the calculator, which has a large digital readout. The child and parent and I sit down and go through a certain procedure.

CHILD: What are you going to do with that?

ME: I'm going to use it to figure out how many days you've been here on the planet. Let's see here, you just turned six, which means you have been here two thousand, one hundred, and ninety days. Come here and let me show you what a big number that is.

CHILD: Wow!

ME: Now, this is what I want to know. In two thousand, one hundred, and ninety days, how many times have bad guys or ghosts or spookies or monsters come into your room and done something bad to you?

CHILD: What?

ME: How many times in the two thousand, one hundred, and ninety days have bad guys or ghosts or spookies or monsters gotten you?

CHILD: Well, none I guess.

ME: We don't do "I guess" when it comes to important things like this. I really want you to tell me how many times they have come into your room and done something bad to you.

CHILD: None.

ME: Are you sure?

CHILD: You're being silly!

ME: I am indeed. But look, this is what I want you to understand. If the bad guys or ghosts or monsters or spookies have not come into your room and done something bad to you in two thousand, one hundred, and ninety days, what are the chances that anything bad is going to happen?

CHILD: Not much, I guess. Oops. I mean, not much.

ME: OK, let me ask your mom a question. How old are you?

MOM: I'm thirty-three and a half.

ME (to the child): Wow, now we're going to see some really big numbers on this calculator. Let's see here, that would be, oh my goodness, your mom has been here on the planet twelve thousand, two hundred, and thirty-two days!

CHILD: Wow!

ME: Now, I want you to ask your mom in twelve thousand, two hundred, and thirty-two days how many times she has had bad guys or ghosts or monsters or spookies come into her room and do something bad to her.

CHILD: Mom?

MOM: Never. Not even once.

ME: And by the way, I want you to ask your mom how many times in twelve thousand, two hundred, and thirty-two days she has seen a real story in the newspaper or the news on television where they showed pictures of a real monster or a real ghost or a real spookie.

CHILD: Mom?

MOM: Never. Not even once.

CHILD: But I saw some on TV. Brandon was watching something.

MOM: Sweetie, those were make-believe, like really fancy Halloween costumes. They weren't really real.

CHILD: Brandon said they were.

MOM: He was just teasing you. They weren't really real.

CHILD: OK.

ME: But I just have to check to make sure about all of this. Did anything bad happen to you last night?

CHILD: Nope.

ME: How about the night before that?

CHILD: Nope.

ME: And the night before that?

CHILD: No, you silly!

ME: Night before that?

CHILD: No!

ME: Before that?

CHILD: No!

ME: Before that and before that and before that and before that?

CHILD: No, no, no, no, no, no!

ME: Are we really going to have to go through all of your two thousand, one hundred, and ninety nights?

CHILD: No!

ME: OK, I guess you win. So what have you learned about how safe you are in your house?

CHILD: I'm safe!

ME: So what are you going to say to yourself tonight before you go to bed?

CHILD: I'm going to tell myself that I'm safe and nothing is going to get me.

ME: And are you going to remember your numbers and think about how many days you've been here on the planet and everything has turned out great?

CHILD: Yes.

ME: Good for you!

During discussions such as this, it is important to find out what the child is using as proof that something bad will happen. If he has had truly bad things happen in the past, such as the house catching on fire or being in an automobile accident, it is important to acknowledge that indeed bad things do happen, but just because a bad thing happened once does not mean that it will happen again and again, which is often what children who have been harmed assume.

It is also important to remember that children can get horribly spooked by the bad things they see on TV. If a child is kidnapped in a distant state, over the next few weeks my office fills up with anxious children. They believe when they see it on TV that it is happening everywhere, even in their neighborhoods, and that it has a high probability of happening to them. Again, in situations like this, I go night by night by night with them to attempt to show them that they live in a safe house and a safe neighborhood.

Simulations

Remember Steven, the boy we met in chapter 1 who would attack other children at the bus stop because it seemed to him that he simply had to be the first one on the bus? He is a good example of another type of anxious child. He was not particularly perfectionistic. He did not have the highly focused safety fears about death and dying and bad guys and monsters that some kids have. He did not fit the full criteria for OCD, but he was very rigid and unyielding once he got something in his head.

We can tell children like Steven that we need to talk with them about how they should respond in a certain situation, and they will nod their heads and try to change the subject as quickly as possible. When we call them on it, they will insist that they know what to do and that there is no reason to talk about it any further. This shows just how anxious they are. Talking about the situation provokes such strong emotions that they try to shut down the talk immediately.

With Steven, I first used a talk-based cognitive therapy focused on the point that nothing bad could conceivably happen to him if he failed to be the first one on the bus. He never could say exactly why he had to be first. It was just what his brain told him, as he explained it.

We talked about the idea that a guy's own brain can fool him, an idea that he seemed to like, and he integrated it into his thinking. He also liked the idea of using the brain game that I talked about in chapter 2. He told me that he thought his little kid brain had fooled him into thinking that he had to be the first one on the bus and that now his big kid brain realized that this was a silly idea.

I also used several exposure-based procedures with Steven. With some children, I have to literally teach their brains not to go on red alert by exposing them over and over to the event that typically blasts them into orbit. One procedure I used with Steven was to have him go to the bus lot with his mother and brother and practice getting on a bus second and third to show him that everything would be just fine. Another time I paid Steven five dollars to wait until last to get on the bus to show him that nothing bad would happen. Steven ultimately did well and came to see the flaws in his thinking. He had ample issues to address because of his tendency to think in rigid patterns, but assaulting other kids was no longer one of them.

If your child is a worried exploder, you will get nowhere with punishments and consequences. Her worries, more than anything else, demand that you spend time with her in order to help her feel safe and overcome the fears that so dominate her mind. Ultimately, you should be thankful when your child tells you what is worrying her, because it means that she is looking to you for a solution. This is a sign of trust, an indication that you have managed to do more than a few things right. Remember that there are children out there who never tell anyone about their fears and who grow up to be fearful adults with lives dominated by the fact that they just don't feel safe.

If your child is a worrier, you should also get him or her into treatment with someone who works primarily with children and who has a strong interest in childhood anxiety. All of the professionals who work with you and your child should have some understanding of both cognitive therapy and exposure therapy, as the two can make a powerful combination. Should you need to turn to medication, it is of the utmost importance that you work with a physician whose primary business is treating children, typically a child psychiatrist or a pediatrician or neurologist with a special interest in childhood psychological issues.

8

MAYBE I'M DEPRESSED

*

IF YOU'RE SEARCHING for a hot topic in child psychology and child psychiatry, you're in the right chapter. There are few issues more riveting than diagnosing young children with bipolar disorder. It is a black hole of a subject, powerful enough to suck up all of the attention of parents and professionals and researchers, so powerful indeed that it tends to make us forget about all the other reasons behind cranky, agitated, explosive behavior. Anyone who works with children is inundated with questions such as "My kid blows up all the time — could he be bipolar?"

Bipolar Disorder in Children

The stereotypes we have of bipolar disorder are of adults swooping between manic, giddy highs and "valley of the shadow of death" lows. In their early hypomanic states, bipolar adults feel great and believe that their minds are working with unusual clarity. For some it can be a period of sustained creativity and productivity. However, if they progress into full-blown mania, things go bad quickly. They begin to care little about sleep, can go on remarkable spending sprees, and become grandiose to the point of being delusional about their own powers and abilities. In some cases, the mania subsides and they edge back into darkness. Their moods crash onto the bleakest of shores, from which they can see no tomorrow. Psychological folklore is full of stories of manic individuals who have died because they refused to sleep or eat and literally burned themselves out, or who took their own lives because they just could not keep going through all the ups and downs any longer.

Have we come to the point where we believe that this horrible disorder is not limited to adults but can also affect children? Yes we have. But just as with other forms of depression, there are large differences between pediatric bipolar disorder and its adult versions.

In the debate over whether or not young children can have bipolar disorder, two issues are hotly contested. The first is whether or not children experience mania, a question that lies at the very root of the disorder. Diagnostic purists insist that you cannot have bipolar disorder in the absence of observable periods of mania. The second issue is whether or not frequent, highly agitated moods are an indicator of bipolar disorder.

The issue of mania in children has been addressed in an important study by Joan Luby and Andy Belden of Washington University. They examined thirteen core symptoms of mania (irritability, extreme elation, grandiosity, high levels of talk, racing thoughts, flight of ideas, decreased sleep, motor pressure, unusual levels of activity, unusual levels of energy, uncontrolled laughing, uninhibited gregariousness, and hypersexuality) in a group of 303 children ages three to six. They found that the bipolar children were significantly more likely to display these core symptoms than the healthy children in the group.

As useful as such findings are, you should be aware of just how difficult it can be to get an accurate diagnosis for your child and how difficult it can be for a mental health specialist or physician without special expertise to diagnose this disorder. For example, a review of the records of twenty-six children ages three to seven who were diagnosed with bipolar disorder by psychiatric experts at the Cincinnati Children's Hospital Medical Center found that none had received that diagnosis by their own referring physicians. The most common diagnoses made by their doctors were ADHD and oppositional defiant disorder. In addition to teaching us about the difficulty of making an accurate diagnosis, this study shows how easy it is for a child to receive the wrong diagnosis, which implies that he will receive the wrong treatment, which in turn may impede his return to health for years.

Let's put the issue of mania aside for a moment and return to the issue of agitated moods. It is extreme irritability, not mania, that most often lands a child in a psychiatric hospital. The irritability of bipolar children is legendary, generally agreed to be several steps beyond what is typically seen in most children. These children strike others as *extremely* explosive or *absolutely* out of control or *severely* angry. There seems to be a bipolar type of agitation that is just not seen in other disorders, so its existence might be taken as a cardinal sign of the disorder. But there is no general agreement on this point. Diagnostic purists would say that highly agitated behavior in the absence of a period of mania does not equal bipolar disorder, even though there is an increasing tendency for children to be diagnosed with bipolar disorder and treated with medications because of their agitation.

Research at the National Institute of Mental Health examined this issue of irritability in two groups of children ages ten to fifteen, along with a contrast group of children who had no diagnosis. One group fit the criteria for a relatively new diagnostic category, referred to as severe mood dysregulation (SMD). Children with this diagnosis display high levels of irritability that are not episodic and not accompanied by periods of euphoric mood. The second group fit the criteria for what is broadly accepted to indicate childhood bipolar disorder—having a history of at least one manic or hypomanic episode with a euphoric mood. The subjects were placed in an experiment designed to frustrate them, and their brain wave patterns were monitored during the frustration task. As anticipated, the children in both of the diagnostic categories became significantly more emotionally aroused during the frustration task than the contrast group. However, there were major differences in brain wave patterns between the bipolar group and the SMD group, indicating that these are two separate disorders.

The implications of this for clinical practice are that low frustration tolerance and high levels of irritability are in and of themselves not necessarily indicative of bipolar disorder, particularly if they are not episodic in nature. If you suspect that your exploding child has bipolar disorder, it is best to have him or her examined by someone who is thoroughly familiar with it and who is skilled in making the distinctions between bipolar disorder, chronic highly irritated mood, oppositional defiant disorder, conduct disorder, and ADHD. There is not yet enough known about SMD to determine whether it should be treated with the same medications used to treat bipolar disorder.

Meet Jody

Let me tell you about an adopted ten-year-old girl who could be the poster child for all of the confusion and pain that a family is likely to go through in an attempt to arrive at an accurate diagnosis and appropriate treatment. Jody's parents described her as highly oppositional, explosive, and prone to be mean and angry for no apparent reason. She was assaultive toward her brother and had been known to scratch his face seriously, had slammed his hand in the door on purpose, and had pushed him down a flight of stairs. Trips in the car with her became dreaded events because she would always stir up something, which of course she would blame on someone else. She would get into intense fights and arguments with her brother when they were visiting relatives, something her parents understandably found to be embarrassing. Her behavior had pushed the family to the breaking point, and the parents had seriously considered breaking the girl's adoption and returning her to foster care. The negative impact that this could have on her psychologically was almost unthinkable.

There were a number of important questions to consider when

pondering the underlying cause, or causes, of her explosive behavior. First of all, she was psychologically touchy and reactive. If you even hinted that something she did might be wrong, it would set her off on a course of intense weeping and wailing about how mean the world was to her. In this regard, her mood could shift so rapidly that it was breathtaking. What did this mean? Did it mean that she was highly defended and did not have the personal strength to admit to any faults or mistakes? Was she suffering from some form of agitated depression? Did it mean that she was bipolar?

Additionally, she had no insight into the impact of her behavior on others. Because of this, she had no friends. Did being bounced around to numerous foster homes early in her life stunt her social development? Did it mean that others found her just too cranky, explosive, and unpredictable to play with? She would consistently deny that she had done any of the assaultive behaviors that resulted in injuries to her brother. It was known that her earlier foster parents had been physically abusive to her, so was she acting out her rage about this on others?

I asked her parents to have her examined by a child psychiatrist. I explained to them that in addition to the counseling we were engaged in, it was possible that she would benefit from mood-stabilizing medication. Her parents scheduled the appointment, which, given the shortage of child psychiatrists, took about a month to get. During that time, they continued to fret over the serious possibility of breaking the adoption, an issue that dominated their minds, wrecked their sleep, and left them wondering how their desire to help this child could have gone so awry.

Fortunately, this story has a happy ending. Jody went to see the child psychiatrist, who decided to try a mood-stabilizing medication commonly used in the treatment of bipolar disorder. Its effect on her was relatively immediate and beneficial. Does this mean that we don't have to continue to address the other important issues in her life—her poor social skills and lack of friends, her contentious relationship with her brother, and the effect of abuse at the hands of foster parents who should have been there to protect her? Absolutely not. We will have to continue with those issues for some time. Yet by using medication to treat her mood, we now have a much more stable platform to work from.

Childhood Depression

As compelling an issue as bipolar disorder is, we cannot afford to forget other types of depression that visit children and lay waste to mood and motivation. There is reason to remain alert and alarmed. Depressed children sometimes grow into suicidal teenagers and adults, and it appears that being depressed as a child increases the risk of being depressed as an adult by 400 percent.

Rarely do we think of little children as being depressed. Back in the 1950s, for example, the theoretical notion was that depression was an illness of the ego. Since children had not aged sufficiently to have a fully functioning superego — that part of the mind that is critical and punishing and prone to pound on the poor ego — it was impossible for them to be depressed. Thankfully, we see past such theory-bound thinking today and are willing to use a bit more common sense when thinking about the psychological lives of children.

What are the criteria for diagnosing depression in children? WebMD (www.webmd.com) alerts us to the following signs of childhood depression.

- Frequent sadness, tearfulness, and/or crying
- Hopelessness
- Decreased interest in activities or inability to enjoy previously favorite activities
- Persistent boredom; low energy
- Social isolation; poor communication

- Low self-esteem and guilt
- Extreme sensitivity to rejection or failure
- Increased irritability, anger, or hostility
- Difficulty with relationships
- Frequent complaints of physical illnesses such as headaches and stomachaches
- Frequent absences from school or poor performance in school
- Poor concentration
- A major change in eating and/or sleeping patterns
- Talk of or efforts to run away from home

While such guidelines are useful when talking about depression in general, they don't tell us enough about children and the way they get depressed. What else should we look for? There is evidence to suggest that depressed girls are actually more like depressed adults in their self-descriptions due to self-directed hostility. They engage in high levels of self-blame and suffer from low levels of self-esteem, symptoms generally associated with adults. Boys, by contrast, show lower levels of self-directed hostility than girls but basically as much anger, indicating perhaps that they blame their difficulties on people or events outside themselves.

Here are some of the issues that I frequently see in the children I work with who are depressed and that I look for when I suspect depression.

- Blows up and explodes with little actual provocation
- Shows little interest in doing the things that other children enjoy doing, absent any noticeable anxiety about attempting the activities, and absent any concerns about his or her development

- Rarely laughs or seems overly serious
- Is highly critical of others or always describes other children in negative terms
- Does not attempt to engage other children in conversation
- Frequently expresses that other children are smarter, stronger, faster, better artists, and so on
- Frequently says things such as "I'm dumb" or "I'm no good at anything"
- Isolates herself from other children, refuses to join in the group, or expresses the belief that no one likes her or everybody hates her
- Gives up easily in competition or makes excuses in order not to compete
- Acts sad for no apparent reason or cries for no apparent reason
- Voices the opinion that death would be preferable to his or her current existence
- Uses vague complaints of illness to avoid school, sports, or other activities involving interacting with others

The list could, of course, go on and on, and should serve only as a place to start. In general, if you are not seeing your child get into the mix with other children (and do so in a way that makes it obvious that he is having fun), if he feels insecure and unaccepted among his peers, and if he is pessimistic about being successful in his little world, you should consider that your child might be depressed.

In my book *The Depressed Child,* I pose this question: "What is depression for?" I find this to be an interesting issue, believing as I do that the answer is that depression is a feedback loop. Depression is a signal that something deep and complex is amiss in the child's life. I suggest that when we see indications of depression, we need to consider three possible categories of underlying causes. The first is biochemistry. Often there are biochemical forces driving a chronically depressed mood or biochemical reasons for a major depression—the type of depression that suddenly flattens you like a boulder dropped out of an airplane. There is little serious dissention that childhood bipolar disorder, discussed earlier in this chapter, is biochemically based, as opposed to being caused by psychological trauma or life events. Parents are exceptionally aware of this cause of depression and frequently ask if there is a test for it. Sad to say, there is no commercially available test.

Second, other things happening inside a person's mind can create a depressed mood. Children who harbor intense negative thoughts and beliefs about themselves ("I'm stupid," "No one likes me," or "I'm ugly") will invariably find themselves in a depressed state. What they believe about themselves may be far from the truth, according to any reasonable observer, but the depression that such thinking creates is quite real.

Third, things happening outside children can make them depressed: too much stress at school; peer rejection; unstable family situations; hostile, overly critical, or overly controlling parents; lack of emotional warmth in the home—the list is virtually endless.

Searching for Biochemical Causes

Whether you are a parent or a child-care professional, you must learn how to recognize when explosive behavior should be seen as a signal that a child is undergoing a biochemical-based depression. While getting appropriate treatment for your child is obviously always important, in this case diagnostic errors can have lasting consequences. Consider, for example, what might happen if a child is depressed but is showing few symptoms of it other than being consistently out of sorts and explosive, then gets misdiagnosed as being oppositional. For the child, this is a nightmare scenario. She does not feel good physically and emotionally and is in desperate need of something that can heal her mood disorder. Instead, she is likely to be grounded by her parents and lose privileges, when in truth she has no control over how she feels and little control over how she behaves. To such a child, punishments only reaffirm what she already believes, which is that the world stinks and no one is likely to treat her well. In such a situation, depression deepens, and deepens considerably.

My experience is that children who are cranky and explosive because they are undergoing a biochemically based depression (keep in mind that we are talking generally about children in the first grade and up) may be able to tell you that they don't feel good, but they will not be likely to give you any reason why this is the case. To them, it is all a mystery, because nothing has happened that they can put their finger on. You can ask them about any conceivable cause of depression—such as things going bad at home; getting picked on at school; having trouble with their schoolwork; recent losses, setbacks, or failures; their answers will typically be the same: "I don't know."

They are telling you the truth. They are totally unaware of any factor that may be causing them to feel the way they do, and clearly they do not have the ability to tell you that they feel the way they do because they have an imbalance in the neurotransmitters in their brains.

If you believe that your child is undergoing a biochemically based depression, you need to quickly seek the help of a child psychiatrist who is skilled in treating depression. There is consistent evidence that a depressed child who is treated with the appropriate medication can make a rapid recovery—more rapid than if using counseling/psychotherapy alone—and that the combination of medication and cognitive behavior therapy can restore a child to normal functioning at a faster rate than medication alone or counseling alone.

At the same time, it is also important to avoid thinking that antidepressants are silver bullets. About 40 percent of the people who take them do not seem to respond to them. Of the approximately 60 percent who do respond, some experience significant side effects. Others respond just as well to a placebo as they do to an antidepressant. Also be aware that the use of SSRI medications might actually increase suicidal ideation in some young people who take them. This issue is far from being resolved, because inadequate research attention has been paid to medication use in children. Some results indicate that antidepressants that work with adolescents do not work with younger children. In addition, some results indicate that in adolescents, the suicide rate has actually decreased as SSRI use has increased, but I am unaware of any such statistics regarding younger children.

The Power of Beliefs

We cannot underestimate the power of one's own beliefs to create depression. I once worked with a precocious eleven-year-old girl who would frequently explode and yell at her mother, seemingly over nothing. She had always refused to talk about what was bothering her, but in my office one day, she screamed at her mother, "Don't you get it? I hate myself!" Her issues, once out, were numerous: she saw herself as too fat, as not pretty enough, as someone that no boy would ever be interested in. She told me that she wanted a T-shirt that said I SUCK.

It is too bad that we can't read minds. If we could, we would be much quicker to understand the thoughts and feelings behind depressive explosions and to offer these children help well in advance of the onset of a depressed mood. In lieu of this, we have to listen closely to what a child says about herself in relation to her peers, siblings, and other family members, particularly when she does explode. Sometimes the truth comes tumbling out during these outbursts, and we'd better be listening if we really want to help.

Children, over years of interacting with their parents, siblings, peers, and teachers, develop secret "truths" about themselves—judgments about their worth and value as human beings in comparison to the people they know, particularly their classmates. Depressed children almost invariably compare themselves to other children in a way that leaves them feeling inferior, and this inferiority becomes their main private truth about themselves. They rarely reveal it to others, because it is so hot, so radioactive, and so painful to approach that it just seems better to bury it. It goes without saying, however, that this truth continues to cook in the background, desiccating the child from the inside out.

Other ways that depressed children think also can be harmful to them in the long run. It has long been known that some depressed individuals suffer from what has been termed "learned helplessness." They tend to believe that the negative events in their lives are due to their own inadequacies and that, in turn, these inadequacies will affect all areas of their lives. They believe that this cycle is unlikely to change, ever. Conversely, they attribute their successes to luck or to chance and believe that they have no control over their lives.

It is legitimate to raise the question as to whether or not cognitive behavior therapy can be done with young children. One of the demands of this type of therapy is that the child must be able to understand the difference between a thought, a feeling, and a behavior. He will have to be able to see how negative thoughts or feelings can create negative behaviors, negative feelings can create negative thoughts, and so on. Developmental theory suggests that children cannot engage in abstract reasoning until around the age of eight, and there is evidence showing that children in the seven- to eight-year-old range are as capable of distinguishing thoughts from feelings as children in the ten- to eleven-year-old range. Other evidence shows that five-year-olds are much less aware of their own thoughts than eight-year-olds, suggesting that attempts to use complex cognitive therapy with young children may prove unproductive.

My own experience had led me to believe that very young children, those in the three- to six-year-old range, who appear to be depressed respond much better to changes in their structure and environment than to traditional talk-oriented therapy. It is best to make sure that such children are consistently exposed to enjoyable events, given tons of physical attention (holding, hugging, and cuddling), and given lots of opportunities to talk about the things that bother and worry them (from monsters and ghosts in the closet to fears of being left behind, getting lost, or not being loved).

It is quite likely that the additional time and attention it will take to engage children in talk about these issues is actually curative to both child and parent. For instance, Vicky Flory, an Australian researcher, taught the parents of eleven depressed children to be more empathetic during their interactions with their children. This resulted in both a decrease in child depression and a decrease in parenting stress.

The Impact of External Forces

Sometimes it is neither neurotransmitters nor self-concept that causes a child to be depressed. Sometimes it is what the world is doing to the child. For example, I know a fantastic nine-year-old boy, Seth, who recently exploded at another child at a birthday party. The child, who was popular among the other kids in the neighborhood, had berated Seth and degraded him in every possible public situation for months. He was one of the reasons Seth was in counseling. At the party, the boy told Seth in front of the other boys that he sucked at sports and couldn't throw a football right. Seth told the kid that he might suck at football, but he didn't suck at martial arts, which he had quietly been learning over the past few months. You can guess the ending of this story.

Seth had become the classic victim of that dynamic in bullying situations in which all the other kids join with the bully to make fun of a child in hopes that the bully won't turn on them instead. Once Seth demonstrated to everyone that he was no longer a safe target, his life improved immeasurably.

My main job with him had initially been to listen as he vented his frustrations over being picked on and to come up with ways to deal with it. I suggested that he take a martial arts course in hopes of increasing his confidence level. After his victory, my job was to listen to him talk about how to handle himself in future situations. Good kid that he is, he came to the conclusion that he cannot beat up all the bullies in the world. He has learned that he can walk away from such situations, but now he has that special satisfaction of knowing that he does not have to run away in fear.

Some children, however, do have to learn to run away, and they deserve our clear attention and help. Those who are chronically targeted for bullying are often physically small, have poor social skills and low self-esteem, and have been abandoned by their peers — all of which makes them inviting targets. The world these children occupy can seem uniformly hostile for clear reasons. Can there be any confusion over the fact that such children will sometimes blow up over something seemingly small because they are so frustrated with what life is doing to them every day? Sometimes the straw does indeed break the camel's back.

Physical complaints can sometimes tip us off to the fact that bad things are happening to our children. There is an interesting published case of a boy who was quick to anger and yelled at his mother frequently. His grades were dropping rapidly, and once or twice a week, he complained of abdominal pain. On occasion, his physical complaints resulted in his being sent home from school. While it may have been tempting to label this boy as oppositional due to his behavior toward his mother, further examination found that he was being bullied at school and because of this was depressed. You should always be suspect of cranky behavior paired with vague physical symptoms and avoidance of situations or activities that your child used to do easily. This is sometimes a signal that depression has descended over your child and must be addressed immediately.

There are several other things you should think about if you are dealing with an explosive child and you believe that the cause of the child's explosive behavior is hidden depression.

First, depressed children frequently resist talking, not because they don't want help, but because they are hesitant to reveal what they truly think about themselves or are ashamed of their behavior. At the same time, they know that they cannot get well all by themselves. They will fight you tooth and nail about giving them the help they so desperately desire. You must remain persistent, and you must insist that they attend counseling with someone who specializes in children and who has the training and background to help depressed children.

Second, children in the three- to five-year-old range are not particularly self-reflective, and because of this, they are not likely to exhibit the type of depression in which the main symptom is a poor self-concept or self-hatred. They respond best to hugs, holding, reassurance, and making sure they know what is going to happen, when, and who it involves. Self-concept-related depression seems to occur in older children, those age six and up, who are increasingly able to notice their own flaws and who increasingly become sensitive to the negative things others say to them. "Proof" that a child is inferior, unlikable, or ugly can come from all directions. There are too many bad kids and abusive adults who are more than happy to demean a child, threaten her, and provide her with every conceivable reason to think badly of herself because of the perverse pleasure it brings them. Ultimately, however, proof comes simply from the fact that over time, the child comes to see herself as inferior: "If I believe it, it must be so."

Third, depressed children almost always have double standards. The flaws that a depressed child uses as proof of his inferiority are the exact same everyday shortcomings that other people have as well. Depressed children are quite forgiving of these flaws in others but see themselves as inferior human beings for having them. You must point out to them that they should be equally forgiving of themselves.

Finally, you cannot know what your child is using as proof against himself unless you ask. Talking to a child is the only way adults have of reading a child's mind, and it requires scheduling face-to-face time on a regular basis. Start the process simply by saying, "I've been wondering lately how you have been feeling about yourself." You will be surprised how far that comment can take you.

9

IT SEEMS LIKE EVERYONE LEARNS FASTER THAN ME

IMAGINE NOT BEING ABLE to get information to go into your brain, despite the fact that you are not the type of kid to give up and will labor for hours over a paragraph that other kids can read in minutes. Also imagine that you are smart and want to grow up to be a scientist who invents medicines that make old people well. Add this to the mix: everyone around you thinks you are stupid because you just got kicked out of the fourth grade for the second year in a row at the alternative school for children with severe behavior problems. If you can imagine all of this, you will know exactly what it's like to be Franklin.

He calmly explained his latest expulsion to me. It was over refusing to give his teacher a ruler that he was playing with during instruction. When his teacher attempted to take it away from him, he hit her. Another staff member stepped in, picking him up to restrain him. However, the staff member stood too close to a wall. Franklin put his feet on the wall for leverage and shoved hard enough to send himself and the staff member backward over a desk. All of this must have looked like a scene from a bad movie to anyone who was watching.

I scheduled Franklin to come in for testing. The results of his achievement test showed that he was reading at grade level 2.8, or the eighth month of second grade. He was supposed to be in the fifth grade, so his reading level was roughly half of what would be expected for someone his age. Then I gave Franklin a test that measures listening comprehension, one that is not biased by reading difficulties. His score was 8.1, or the first month of eighth grade.

Several key points have emerged since Franklin completed the testing. It is objectively clear that he is very bright but has a marked reading disorder. The more I talk to him, the more aware I am that his fighting, arguing, explosions, disruptive behavior, and clowning are actually attempts to prevent his teachers and peers from knowing that he can't read.

If you have a child who pitches a fit every morning about going to school, you may think that something is amiss at the school. Is he getting picked on or bullied? Is he bored or unchallenged? Does he simply dislike anything to do with academics? We all know kids who are as happy as a clam as long as they are left to putter around, or play with toys, but who turn into explosive devices when it's time to get out the math work sheets or the reading assignments.

Maybe something else is going on. Maybe your child has a learning disability, something that affects an enormous number of school-age children. Approximately 2.8 million American public school children receive special education services for learning disabilities, a figure that represents almost 6 percent of all the children enrolled in the system.

In this chapter, I will focus on the emotional toll that learning disabilities can take on a child's life. In particular, I will attempt to show why learning disabilities may be the hidden cause of explosions that occur at school or during homework time. I will also try to leave you with some basic ideas about what you can do to help your child overcome a learning problem.

What Are Learning Disabilities?

Learning disabilities are neurologically based difficulties with mastering certain types of material or activities. They arguably have nothing to do with intelligence, although they have a massive impact on a child's achievement, ability to learn new material, enjoyment of the learning process, and test performance. They also have a huge impact on an individual's life success.

The website of the Learning Disabilities Association of America (www.ldaamerica.org) states that there are four areas of mental operations that, when disrupted, create learning difficulties. These are *input,* the ability of the brain to take in information of various types, such as visual or auditory information; *integration,* the ability of the brain to organize and make sense of the information it has received in a way that allows it to be used to solve problems; *memory,* the ability to retain and recall information; and *output,* the ability to communicate information through a variety of means, such as spoken language, writing, drawing, and constructing.

When learning disabilities are thought of in such terms, it rapidly becomes obvious that most of us have small disabilities of some sort. Chances are that you have something you do not do well compared to your other skills. My aversion to algebra and trig is likely based on the fact that for most of my life, it has been hard for me to remember all of the steps necessary to work long equations. I remember taking a physics class in college, believing that I might learn something about the beginning of the universe, the nature of time, and what might happen if we could shoot an object through a black hole without it getting crushed. Instead, the professor found a way to make a potentially fascinating subject exceptionally boring. This is my recollection of one of the questions on our final exam: If a truck that weighs 4,800 pounds and is headed east at 73 miles per hour has a head-on collision with a 2,950-pound car that is headed west at 63 miles per hour, which vehicle will be displaced off the road, how far, and how much energy will be released? I answered it like this: "I don't care." This was certainly a truthful statement, but moreover was indicative of my inability to sequence my way through such a math problem. (I should also note that I do not recall my professor being amused.)

However, it is not the small learning disabilities like mine that parents need to worry about. It is the large ones like Franklin's, the ones that bedevil parents because they know intuitively that their child is bright, the ones that frustrate children so thoroughly that even the thought of school fills them with dread.

Why Children with Learning Disabilities Explode

Let's look at the world through the eyes of a child with another type of learning disability. Let's pretend that *you* have what is known as a "demand language" difficulty. Children with an output disorder like this may have a head full of knowledge that they love to share—as long as they decide in advance what they want to talk about. But if you ask them a question when they do not anticipate being asked anything, you will see them shut down like a nuclear reactor on red alert. The reason for this is that it takes them much longer than you might guess to access their memory for information and to get it properly sequenced in an order that will make sense when it is finally spoken. That is what it feels like.

TEACHER (looking at you): Please tell us what you learned about King Tut at the museum yesterday.

(Your heartbeat is escalating. No words are coming out of your mouth, but this is what is going on in your head: Lord Carnarvon. Door to tomb was patched. He was thirteen. Gold mask. Howard Carter found it. Jars with the brain and heart and liver. Lots of loaves of dried-up bread. Purple flower his wife gave him? A chariot. Two statues guarding the doorway, painted black. Where to start? Where?)

TEACHER (tapping her toe and looking impatient): Did you hear my question?

(Still no words come out of your mouth. Other children are beginning to snicker. Someone off to your left whispers, "Stoooo-piddd.")

There is yet another child you should know about with an output disorder. He cannot spell his name out loud. He can write it with no problem and can read it with no problem. This may seem like no big deal to you, but put yourself in his position for a moment. His last name is unusual, nothing at all like Smith or Jones, and people are always asking him to spell it for them. But he can't. Imagine the looks he gets and what others think about this perfectly bright, enjoyable young man.

Claude, by contrast, has no difficulty getting words out of his mouth. He knows everything there is to know about dinosaurs—what era they flourished in, what habitat they needed, what they ate, how much they weighed, how tall they were, and on and on. He can talk at great length about this, with impressive detail. But Claude cannot write a paragraph about dinosaurs if his life depended on it. He has great difficulty with written expressive sequencing. (The fact that he can speak at length about dinosaurs tells us that he has no difficulty with spoken sequencing.) It boils down to this: If he is allowed to say it, he can tell you a lot about many things. If he has to write it, he agonizes over where to begin and how to present things in an order that makes sense. He frequently explodes and rips up his papers. His trouble extends to almost all forms of writing, from single-sentence answers to lengthy reports presented on poster board. When you think about what life must be like for him—his head crammed full of interesting facts that he can't use on written tests and papers—you shouldn't be surprised that he explodes so often.

If you think I am exaggerating the effects of these disorders, read this letter from an eighth-grade boy I work with who also has marked difficulty getting the words out of his mouth.

> If I could be anything I would be a knife so I could kill the people that are pissing me off and to get out of this horrible class and all these freakin butthole kids and to kill all the teachers that get on my nerves and then be a torch and burn everyone that called me stupid and then a bomb to destroy this crappy school with Roaches going through the walls and by roaches I mean kids.

Letters like this need little explanation, but they should remind us that while we are relatively quick to understand that a learning disability can make classroom work and homework academically difficult, we are sometimes blind to the emotional toll these difficulties take on kids. Children with learning disabilities blow up out of sheer frustration and embarrassment. It is important to remember that they are often keenly aware of their problems. They frequently suspect themselves of being stupid, so when someone else says such things within their earshot, it serves as a confirmation of their own beliefs.

How Can We Help Children with Learning Disabilities?

Thankfully, there are so many techniques available for helping children with learning disabilities that they fill entire books. In this section, I barely scratch the surface of the options available.

Play to Their Strengths

From the perspective of a child psychologist who is just as concerned with self-concept as he is with learning how to diagram sentences or mastering quadratic equations, I can tell you that it is exceptionally important to make sure your child is aware of all the successful people who have learning disabilities. Does your child like fashion? So does Tommy Hilfiger, who has dyslexia. Sports? So does Terry Bradshaw, the Super Bowl–winning quarterback for the Pittsburgh Steelers and now a successful TV commentator, who has ADHD. Learning disabilities did not stop the Scottish Formula One racecar driver Jackie Stewart from winning three world driving titles. All of these names were found at SchwabLearning.org, a website sponsored by Charles Schwab, the stockbroker who has managed to do OK for himself despite his own learning disabilities, as have actors Orlando Bloom, Danny Glover, and Salma Hayek. Such exceptional individuals remind us of how important it is for you to help your child identify his talents and for you to push the idea from early in life that a person must judge himself based on his strengths, not his weaknesses.

You must also push the idea that a person should make her living using the strengths and skills that come naturally to her and that it is not a sign of failure if she doesn't have a Ph.D. in theoretical physics from Stanford or did not go to medical school or law school at Harvard. There are all sorts of ways of being smart, and no one type of intelligence is superior to any other. Such ideas run against society's grain, however, as there is a built-in tendency in schools to ooh and aah over the seventh grader who can work those trig equations in his head but to ignore the kid who has taught himself how to wire a house. When my own children showed this tendency to value one type of intelligence over another, I mentioned that someday in the future when their car wouldn't start, they should call a chemistry major.

Help Them Avoid Stinkin' Thinkin'

You should teach your child everything there is to know about the particular learning disability he or she is dealing with (after you have educated yourself about it). This is based on the notion that the devil you know is preferable to the devil you don't know. As part of teaching your child about what he is struggling with, you should also teach him that there are a number of strategies that he can use to help control his frustration.

One useful strategy is to teach children to monitor the types of thinking that is going on inside their heads as they struggle. It is certainly OK to say "This is hard" or "I'm having trouble with this." These are truthful statements. But when a child's interior messages turn negative, it is like lighting a slow-burning fuse. The more the child says to herself, "I'm stupid" or "I'll never be able to do this," the closer she gets to an explosion. I tell the children I work with that at my house, we refer to such negative thinking as "stinkin' thinkin'," and I get them to understand that the only possible outcome of stinkin' thinkin' is that they will make themselves feel even worse. I ask their moms and dads to look at them and say, "No stinkin' thinkin' allowed" whenever the parents catch the kids thinking negatively.

Children with learning disabilities also frequently respond to their mistakes or poor test scores by punishing themselves. Their typical way of doing this is to call themselves names, often out loud: "You idiot!" or "You dummy!" You can see how such critical self-talk can lead to depression in children with learning disabilities. They can come to feel beaten down, to identify themselves as damaged goods. Children with learning disabilities will often be entirely forgiving of any of their peers who struggle with learning issues and will tell them that their difficulties mean nothing about them as people. However, the same children will use their own struggles as proof of their personal inferiority. It is vitally important that you disrupt this type of thinking with a dose of reality, pointing out that your child is not a giant lump of faults and weaknesses, but a living, breathing human being who certainly has her struggles but also has strengths that cannot be measured by an achievement test. As Einstein so famously said, "Not everything that is important can be measured, and not everything that can be measured is important."

Know What Causes Them to Blow

It goes without saying that it is useful for you to learn to read the signs indicating that your child is about to lose control over issues related to learning disabilities. If you see him beginning to get tense and tight while studying or hear him begin to mutter negative things about himself, a particular class, or a particular teacher, it is time to have him take a break.

If at all possible, you should also find strategies that can be used to eliminate many of the sources of frustration that lead to explosions. For example, approach your child's teacher with the idea of having her work every other math problem on a math work sheet or test. Doing this may reduce her aversion to working math problems, because she will not see math as dominating all of her waking hours.

There is also some evidence that elementary school students with learning disabilities perform better on math tests when problems are shown on a video monitor and read aloud by the teacher as children work them. This procedure does not appear to enhance the performance of students without learning disabilities or middle school students, emphasizing just how important it is to be aware of the early educational needs of children who struggle.

If your child has learning problems that are specific to reading comprehension, you can ask his teacher to have him take multiple-choice tests in a quiet area or to combine the use of a quiet area with having a teacher's aide read the questions and the possible answers aloud to him. While the aide obviously cannot help your child choose the correct answer, he or she can make sure that your child understands what all the words mean and that he understands the question. Without such help, children with reading comprehension difficulties do not get a fair chance to demonstrate their knowledge and understanding of the subject matter. Their poor grades often speak more to their difficulties with reading than to their lack of knowledge.

It is also important to note that some children simply do not test well on multiple-choice or written tests. While schools do not like the idea of testing a child verbally because it is not easy to quantify how many points their answers should receive, it is eminently humane to insist that a child who does not test well be given a chance to respond verbally to each of the test items in a way that can earn her extra points or can be averaged with her performance on the traditional test. This is particularly important for children who have issues with written sequencing. One special education teacher I know tells me there are several students she tests while walking down the hallways and having a conversation. The kids do not even realize that they have been tested.

This suggestion about verbal testing is based on the commonsense notion that there are multiple ways to find out what a child knows, particularly if the child is frustrated and explosive because of his academic struggles. It is exceptionally shortsighted to believe that the only way to measure knowledge is in a written format. Bridget Dalton and her colleagues at Vanderbilt University assessed fourth graders with and without learning disabilities after giving them instruction on electricity. The children performed better on a hands-on test in which they had to use what they had learned than on a written test. Such results indicate that constraining children to written tests may not reveal their true understanding of the subject.

Another important point that comes under the heading of knowing your child well is the issue of whether she is more visually oriented or verbally oriented. With this in mind, it makes sense to test a child who is visually oriented by having her respond to pictures, graphs, or charts or to build, draw, or make something to demonstrate her knowledge. Does your child love videos and games? If so, try to match her with a teacher who uses films, TV programs, and computer-based technologies for instructional purposes. Does she like to move around from one seating area to another as she reads, as opposed to staying in one spot? I know one teacher who puts beanbag chairs in the back of her classroom, and kids can choose to sit in them to read or listen as long as they do not disrupt others. She tells me that for some children, being allowed to move about prevents them from getting so frustrated and antsy that they blow up.

Have Them Tested

Some schools will go along with suggestions like these on an informal basis. Other schools will tell you that they can make compensations for your child only if he has been qualified for special education services. These services range from placing your child in a self-contained classroom with a very low pupil-to-teacher ratio to providing one-on-one help to your child in certain subjects. Children who are found eligible to receive special education services receive an individualized education program (IEP). This identifies the child's specific educational needs and the techniques to be used to help him strengthen his areas of weakness. If his areas of weakness cannot be modified, the IEP also identifies techniques that can be used to compensate for these weaknesses.

You should be aware of the process of getting your child tested by your school system to see if she has any learning disabilities. First, you will need to make a *written* request to have a meeting with the school to determine whether your child qualifies for testing. The school has thirty days to convene this meeting. Such a meeting will typically include you, the child's teachers, the school counselor, a school psychologist, and an administrator who runs the meeting. This meeting is your opportunity to explain why you think that your child needs to be tested. You should go in well prepared with examples of the types of learning problems your child is experiencing. For example, if you suspect a learning disability specific to math, you might bring in samples of work showing consistently poor math grades and consistently good grades in other subjects. Or if you suspect a disability in reading, you might bring in test results showing poor reading comprehension but adequate performance in other subjects. Your child may fit a different pattern, one in which everyone who interacts with her judges her to be bright and capable, but her performance seems to be consistently low for reasons that have nothing to do with poor motivation or lack of effort. This is your opportunity to convince the team that formal testing is necessary to get to the root of the problem. This is *not* your opportunity to complain about a teacher you do not like or to rail against a particular school policy that grinds you.

If the team agrees that your child qualifies for testing, the school has sixty working days to complete the testing. The law also allows you to have your child tested by an outside psychologist at the school's expense. Most schools have a list of psychologists who are qualified to do this type of testing and can provide you with several names.

If your child is tested, you need to have a basic understanding of what the test scores mean in order to talk to the school psychologist or counselor about your child's educational needs. Keep in mind when going over your child's scores that the statistically average percentile score on any test is the 50th percentile. You also need to know that the average range goes from the 25th to the 75th percentile. If your child's percentile scores on a particular test fall between the 25th and 75th percentiles, the child is said to be operating in the average range.

However, keep in mind that if your child scores at the 25th percentile on reading comprehension and your school tells you that he is performing within the average range, approximately 75 out of 100 children will be expected to outperform him on the same test. This does not bode well for his education, regardless of the fact that the school says his performance is within the average range.

Some schools, of course, will be alarmed by such a score and design procedures to help your child improve his reading. Other schools won't budge an inch. One fifth-grade child I worked with years ago had a reading comprehension score at the 18th percentile, meaning that 82 out of 100 children would be likely to outperform him on that test. His IQ score was at the 23rd percentile. He had moved from another school district, where he had qualified for special education services and had done reasonably well. His new district refused to offer him such services, taking the position that since he was not particularly bright to begin with, little more could be expected of him. When I complained, the school responded that the fact that his IQ score and achievement score were so close showed that he was operating at his potential. Never mind that he was sinking like a stone in the regular education program, and never mind that he had told me that he was going to kill himself rather than face more bad grades and retention. The school finally relented and offered him special education services, but only after much arguing and acrimony.

Make a Plan

If you have your child tested by the school and the results indicate that she is below average in any of the areas measured, but not so far below that the school will offer her special services, be prepared to take matters into your own hands. You will have to develop your own plan to help her overcome these difficulties.

While the school may not offer your child special services, it is unlikely to object to a request from you to meet with the school's reading specialist, for example, to pick his or her brain on how to help your child improve his reading comprehension. Likewise for other areas of weakness. Teachers and school-based specialists go into education for a myriad of reasons, one of which is almost always a profound interest in what makes children tick. They are likely to be exceptionally busy but unlikely to turn down your request for a consult.

If the school board's rules prohibit such a consult, you can turn to other community-based resources. Find the local children's multispecialty hospital, which may be affiliated with a university. Such hospitals typically have staff members who specialize in the same learning problems that teachers and school specialists are trained in. In particular, you may want your child to be evaluated by a speech and language therapist, an occupational therapist, a child psychologist, a developmental pediatrician, and/or a child psychiatrist to make sure you get as many informed opinions as possible on how to help him or her learn and adjust to the pressures of the classroom successfully. If your insurance won't cover such services, keep in mind that many large universities offer screening and diagnostic clinics for free and that similar services may be available to you through your local mental health board or health department. Your goal is to learn as much as possible about what is affecting your child's ability to learn and to put together a plan that you can use at home to help her move forward. Surf the Internet, visit bookstores, and get to be on a first-name basis with the owner of the local teacher's supply store.

It is important that we not lose sight of the fact that learning disabilities have unseen emotional costs, and that children who have them tend to blow up and explode due to the frustration of trying to get their brains to do things that their brains are not wired to do. The frustration of children who struggle with learning disabilities becomes a doubled-edged sword that can affect all areas of their lives. Studies of children identified as having learning disabilities have found that as many as half of them also have other social, emotional, and behavioral problems. It is shortsighted to assume that your child is just being lazy if he doesn't want to go to school or that he explodes while doing homework just to be difficult. It is important to remember that children who explode over school-related issues are attempting to escape what causes them the most pain in their young lives. Because of this, it is vitally important to uncover your child's areas of weakness and to devise strategies to help him overcome the weaknesses that are dragging him down emotionally.

10

BUT I LIKE PLAYING WITH THE YOUNGER KIDS

ONE OF THE BASIC TENSIONS between children and adults is the adult's desire for the child to act in a mature manner and the child's desire to simply act, without forethought to consequences. It is a reasonable enough conflict, something most of us experience from both sides of the equation during our lives. The parent's expectations should gently nudge the child forward, increasing competencies, responsibilities, and freedoms as he matures. An immature child doesn't want to be nudged forward by you, me, or anyone else and is prone to blow sky-high when frustrated or placed under demands to act his chronological age.

Children's immature behavior can be characterized along a number of dimensions: They talk in a high-pitched, singsong voice long after their peers have abandoned this affectation. They gravitate toward younger children, preferring the younger children's toys and activities to those of their own age mates. They seem more easily frightened and need more parental reassurance than other children, and they can vastly overreact to cuts, bumps, and bruises. As they age, their peers become increasingly aware of the difference between their own behavior and that of the immature child and sometimes taunt the child by calling her a "baby" or telling her that she is "too little" to play with the other kids.

Curiously, little has been written about immature children and their behavioral patterns. In reading what is out there, you should be especially careful to note the differences between immature children and children who are suffering developmental delays. Immature children have a ceiling to their skills that can go up or down depending on the circumstances. They can talk more maturely when forced or induced to. They can walk in a more mature manner and can grudgingly make themselves interact with their peers. Children with developmental delays do not have this luxury. The ceiling of their abilities is relatively fixed. If they move forward, it is typically at a snail's pace compared to what immature children can achieve.

There does not seem to be any standard medical or psychiatric definition for immature behavior. The types of issues that I see in my work with children who strike their parents and others as immature include the explosive, disruptive, and regressive behaviors I just described. I also tend to see the following types of behaviors in emotionally immature children.

- Are less aware of their own behavior and its impact on others than other children their age. Boys consistently lag behind girls in this regard and should be compared to other boys their age, not to girls.

- Consistently fail to engage in activities or tasks that other children their age do without difficulty, but not due to intellectual or physical limitations.

- Fail to develop the social skills needed to interact successfully with their peers. They try to act "too young" when playing with their peers and may also try to get their peers to act younger or to engage in play that is below their age level.

- Cry easily, get frustrated easily, or explode easily when attempting tasks that they are mentally and physically able to do.
- Act shy, silly, or inhibited in new situations. It may be quite difficult to get them to try anything new.
- Experience mood instability.
- Display poor self-control in groups. Due to this, others tend to avoid interacting with them.
- Constantly perform for others or act cute or funny in an attempt to get others to watch them or pay attention to them. Do not seek the attention of others in an age-appropriate way.

What Can Parents Do?

What can we do to help these children act their age? Let's briefly review the notion of emotional intelligence, based on the work of psychologists John Mayer and Peter Salovey and popularized in the writings of Daniel Goleman in his book *Emotional Intelligence: Why It Can Matter More Than IQ*.

Emotional intelligence is said to comprise four areas of ability. The first, *perceiving emotions*, involves the ability to accurately perceive emotions in the facial expressions and vocalizations of others. Without this ability, there is little chance of understanding others. The second area, *facilitating thought*, is the ability to use the emotions that we have perceived in others to focus our thinking in our dealings with them. The third area, *understanding emotions*, is the ability to use our thinking to develop a reasonable course of action based on what we perceive in others. The fourth area, *managing emotions*, is the ability to remain open to strong emotions, both our own and others', in order to move toward a desirable resolution or goal.

Implicit in this model is that lack of awareness of emotions correlates highly with lack of success in the interpersonal arena, and in other arenas as well. You can see why various schools, organizations, and businesses have seized on this concept to develop training programs for emotional awareness. The results have been impressive. In one study, up to half of the children who completed emotional intelligence training programs showed improved achievement test scores, and more than a third showed improved grades. More important in some ways, children exposed to the training showed improved social behaviors: incidents of misbehavior dropped by an average of 28 percent, suspensions dropped by 44 percent, and other disciplinary actions dropped by 27 percent.

In my own clinical work with children, I have seen how important it is for children (1) to learn to anticipate the impact their behavior might have on others in the future and (2) to learn to understand the impact that they have already had on others in the past. Without at least one of these forms of awareness operating at reasonable levels, there is little chance of their forming mature relationships with others. Children who can't predict will step on the emotional toes of others over and over. Children who lack understanding and empathy after the fact will be seen by others as uncaring and troubled, and possibly even sociopathic.

Meet Jerry

Let me give you an example of working with a child to develop his awareness of the impact he has on others. When I first met Jerry, who was six and in the first grade, he had little to do with his peers, and they had little to do with him. The one time he had tried to play tag with them on the playground, he had gotten tagged quickly. This had sent him into a tearful meltdown. He had screamed repeatedly at the other children that it wasn't "fair" with such vehemence that he had to be picked up and hauled off by his teacher.

His preference at recess was to stay beside the playground monitor or go back into his classroom and be with his teacher. He was frequently found headed toward the part of the playground reserved for the preschoolers, the only children he seemed to be comfortable with. He talked in a singsong cadence, ending each sentence with a lilting upswing of his voice, and had to be constantly reminded to talk like a big boy.

At home, he was easily frustrated and explosive. He still loved to watch Teletubby tapes. He liked to run around the house naked and squealing after his bath and would say that he wished he was still a baby. He had an older brother and sister who also shied away from him because of the way he acted and because of his frequent explosions.

One of the things Jerry's mother could count on was that when she asked him to act like a big boy, he would melt down. He would start to argue that he *was* acting big. He would then whine, huff and puff, fall on the floor, and roll around. His mother would then say, "Eyeballs, please," a command that I use to tell kids that they must make eye contact with me. Once she had his attention, she would say, "What are you making me feel like with your behavior right now?" His first response would usually be "I don't know."

I had told Jerry's mother to reject that response, because in reality it means "Don't make me think" or "I don't want to talk about this." Instead, she should direct him to look at her face, particularly her eyes and her mouth, and try to guess how he was making her feel. At some point, he would indicate that he was making her feel upset, or feel angry. His mother would reply that he was quite accurate in his assessment: "You are right. Your arguing and blowing up is making me upset. As your mom, it is my job to let you know when you are not acting big enough and to help you understand how you should act. I will send you to your room if you do not get control of yourself. What should you do right now?"

"Calm down?"

"Again, you are entirely right. And if you keep blowing up all the time, what are you going to make me and the rest of us think about you?"

This is an important part of training children to understand that their behavior literally teaches others what to think about them. It might have been tempting for Jerry's mom to tell him that he was making his family think that he doesn't act big enough or that he acts too silly too often. However, just coming out with it like that would be guaranteed to activate his defenses, and he would slide into hardy denial. It was much better for his mom to let him come to some reasonable conclusions on his own—to guide him gently, if needed, but also to avoid putting words in his mouth.

At this point, Jerry's response would typically be something like this: "You're all going to think I'm stupid!" The conversation might then proceed as follows:

MOM: No, I think you are a very smart young man. I will never, ever think you are stupid. Guess again, please.
JERRY: You'll think I'm a bad kid.
MOM: Wrong again. I will never think you are a bad kid, even when I don't like how you act. Please take another guess.
JERRY: You'll think I act like a little guy and blow up too much like that stupid Dr. Riley told you to say!
MOM: That's not a nice thing to say. Please say it the right way.
JERRY: You will think I need to act like a big guy.
MOM: That's correct. You want us to think that you are a big kid who controls himself.
JERRY: Shut up, Mom! That's not nice! Leave me alone!
MOM: What is going to happen if you keep on acting like this?
JERRY: Time-out or something stupid like that.
MOM: And if you keep answering me like that, what is going to happen?
JERRY: I'm going to be in bigger trouble.
MOM: You are exactly right again. So, to avoid this trouble, what should you be working on right now?

JERRY: Big guy behavior.
MOM: What about the baby talk?
JERRY: I need to knock it off.
MOM: You've got it again! Now, as they say on *Star Trek*, "Make it so."
JERRY: Huh?
MOM: Work harder on acting big, not exploding, and not using baby talk.
JERRY: OK.

I also instructed Jerry's mother to end each of these interactions with what I refer to as "positive anticipation," which is using what we have learned to anticipate what the consequences will be if we do things correctly. The conversation would go something like this:

MOM: And by the way, if you do a great job at acting like a big guy, not blowing up, and not using baby talk, what do you think will happen?
JERRY: You will buy me a go-cart?
MOM: That's nice to imagine, but try again. What will happen?
JERRY: Everybody will be happier with me.
MOM: Yep. And what will your life be like as long as we are all happy with your behavior?
JERRY: I'll get to do fun stuff.
MOM: Like?
JERRY: Go to Busch Gardens or Water Country USA!
MOM: Yes, that's right. Please work hard.
JERRY: OK.

An interaction like this summarizes many of the things you have to do when talking with any child who is exploding, but in particular with one who is immature. Jerry's mother typically did a fantastic job of remaining calm and in control of herself, even when Jerry descended to new regressive lows in his behavior.

The importance of remaining calm and in control is that immature children do not feel particularly safe to begin with. This is at the root of their behavior. If they felt safe, they would jump freely into interactions with their peers and wouldn't spend so much time wrapped around you. Jerry tried, literally, to wrap his arms around his mother's waist, close his eyes, and bury his face in her rib cage when he walked beside her. It made walking for her quite difficult and did not impress his peers favorably.

Any sense of safety that an immature child does have is entirely tied up in his mother, as you can see with Jerry. A mother is, in the emotional scheme of things, the Rock of Gibraltar, and her child is a balloon that is tethered to her. If the balloon gets punctured, the child will go whizzing all about. However, there is only so far that he can go. If, on the other hand, the mother begins to act emotionally during periods of conflict with an immature child who is clinging and grabbing and regressing because his sense of safety has momentarily disappeared, the tether is cut. There are no limits to how far out of control he might fly. Should this happen, his entire sense of the world will feel threatened, an event guaranteed to make him behave even more immaturely.

The interaction between Jerry and his mother is an example of how to talk with your immature child about her behavior at home. But doing this only in the home environment would be unlikely to help Jerry make progress in the rest of the world. His mother's strategy was to have most of the adults who had close contact with him use the same model of verbal interacting that she used when it came to his immature behavior. Because Jerry was forced to analyze his behavior in a similar manner at home, at school, at his grandparents' house, and elsewhere, he stood a better chance of modifying his immature interactions with others than if he encountered different responses to his behavior in each place. The worst possible situation, of course, would have been for him to encounter no response at all when he was acting his youngest.

Teaching Children How to Interact with Others Outside the Home

In truth, immature children often attempt not to interact with others outside the home. If this is the case with your child, you will have to adopt strategies that will not allow him to avoid consistent contact with his peers and with adults. You might wish to consider the following strategies.

- Keep your child actively involved in group-based activities, such as youth groups at your religious center, clubs, sports, scouting, community organizations, and so on. If she is acting in an immature fashion, quietly pull her aside and give her clear, brief instructions on how she should be acting. Learning interpersonal competencies is a lot like learning to hit a baseball. It is good to talk about it, but it is better to go to the batting cage. Stay upbeat and tell her to give it her best try. Do not hesitate, however, to pull her aside repeatedly if she continues to make the same mistake.
- Watch videos with your child. Choose those that he has already seen, because you will be hitting the pause button frequently and asking what one character was making the other character think or feel, how the offending character should have acted instead, what the offending character is going to make others think about him or her, and so on.
- Go to your child's school without your child knowing you are there. Observe her in her interactions with the other children. Take particular note of whether or not she initiates appropriate interactions and how she responds to others' attempts to interact with her. Debrief your child on your observations later that evening. This will give you lots to talk about.
- Ask your child's teacher to put her in a group leadership role whenever possible to foster appropriate group behavior. She

could be the line leader, hand out materials, call the roll, and so on.

- Ask your child's school counselor if he or she runs "friendship groups" in which children learn to improve their social skills with their peers. If these are available, ask that your child be included.

Playing the Role of Director

Your strategy for working with an immature child should include at its center the awareness that the child is likely to fight you tooth and nail, because insisting that he act in a mature manner forces him into a role that he is not familiar with. Immature children are comfortable with the extremes and do not know any middle ground. Jerry's behavior before treatment oscillated between baby talk and immature play on the one hand and massive meltdowns on the other.

Trying to parent an immature child will force you to clarify your values as a parent, particularly in regard to issues such as how much you should allow a child to express who she is versus how much you should take control of how she acts. It is a razor walk because none of us wants to extinguish a child's personality. At the same time, when she consistently makes poor choices while interacting with others, what should you do? You should get comfortable with the role of director because of the high social stakes at risk. The argument goes like this: If your child's maturity and social perception left her with a clear understanding of how to act in any particular situation, chances are she would be acting appropriately. Your child acts the way she does because her perceptions of how to act are faulty. If allowed to continue to operate out of faulty perceptions, she is bound to alienate others instead of drawing others closer to her in positive, ongoing relationships.

Jerry's mom had to get comfortable with this director role. She knew that there were times with Jerry when the first "take" did not go well and she had to have him redo the behavior, sometimes several times, because his second effort was only a pale attempt at correction—he simply wanted his mom to leave him alone and let him do things his way.

One particular incident in my office illustrates this well. Jerry's mother was sitting in the chair across from my desk. Jerry was sitting in a chair about ten feet away from her. He was playing with a toy car at a moment that he should have been listening, and his mother asked him to give her the car. His initial response was to whine and complain, but eventually he got out of the chair and brought it to her. All of this was appropriate, with the exception of how he walked over to her: He walked leaning well forward, his arms dangling limply at his sides rather than swinging as he walked. He virtually tiptoed over to his mother and then said, "Humph!" when he put the car in her hand. His mother asked him to redo everything, given that the way he had done it was quite infantile. It took him two more tries to get it right—walking in an appropriate manner, making appropriate eye contact with his mother, and skipping the sound effects.

You are likely to find that your child is initially resistant to your director role, which is understandable. However, I have found that children will put more thought into how they look to others and what the outcomes of their behavior will be when they are consistently asked to redo an inappropriate response. In addition, as with any child, you must take the time to praise your child when she spontaneously acts in a mature, appropriate manner. When a child does this, you can bet that she has put some thought into it, even if she cannot describe to you how her thinking has changed. Be sure to reward the effort.

Revisiting Jerry

I had a chance to talk with Jerry's mother alone once we were well under way with his treatment. She told me that Jerry kept her worn-out because she was constantly pushing him to act big. She said that she had accepted the idea that when you have a child like Jerry, you get used to feeling worn-out. In addition to making sure that he acted "big" at home, she ferried him all over the place to keep him involved in group activities so that he could learn to deal with children his own age.

Part of the reason she felt worn-out was because early in our contact, I had asked her to consider placing Jerry in a karate class. I have made this suggestion for many boys whose issues revolve around immaturity, shyness, or being underassertive with their peers. I have yet to see karate turn one of them into a bully, although I have heard of many cases in which it was helpful to a child who learned to contend with hostile and unfriendly peers by staying calm and assertive. Jerry's mother told me that being involved in karate seemed to help Jerry aspire to be more mature. She explained that Jerry's sensei (karate teacher) was someone who obviously relished teaching pride of accomplishment to children and wanted them to have fun. At the same time, he was not the sort to allow immature or inappropriate behavior at his dojo (school), and several times Jerry had to do pushups because he wasn't paying attention or giving his best effort. Jerry felt proud of his uniform and accepted his sensei's rule that he would have to give up his belt if he acted immaturely during class.

Although Jerry's mom was worn-out, I also sensed that she believed that she was worn-out for all the right reasons. She said that a few of the boys at Jerry's school had begun to speak to him in the hallways and that they were starting to mix with him when she took him to school for evening functions. He had stopped trying to stay physically attached to her in places where there were a lot of people or a lot of commotion, situations that always raised his anxiety level. He still had a tendency to stay close to her, but she would shoo him away.

She told me that Jerry had yet to be invited to anyone's house to play, which she and I had established as our ultimate goal. We will consider our work with Jerry to be successful when he gets to that point. It will tell us that he is finally acting in a manner that his peers find acceptable. In pursuit of this goal, Jerry's mother will continue to engage in role plays with him in which his job is to start conversations with another person. She will concentrate on the basics, such as "What is your favorite sport?" or "Have you been to any good movies lately?" It is important to do such drills with immature children in order to improve their social skills. While Jerry has a ways to go before he becomes socially adept, according to his mother his current behavior is much improved over his previous habit of sticking his face right in another child's face and making silly noises in an attempt to win the child's friendship by entertaining him.

While your immature child is likely to resist your efforts to gently nudge her forward, she will be quite proud of herself as her behavior improves. Immature children are like all of the other children we have spoken about thus far in that they want to feel good about themselves and they want the admiration of others. Do not expect this work to go quickly. Telling your child that she must act in a more mature manner is akin to telling her that she must all of a sudden speak fluent German. In fact, the idea of learning a new language is probably an appropriate metaphor for what the immature child must do: learn a few words and phrases every day, until one day she is fluent in the language and no one would ever expect that there had been a problem.

11

MY SOCKS AREN'T RIGHT!

REMEMBER HENRY, the big first grader I told you about in chapter 1 who would punch anyone who brushed against him or bumped into him in line? When I first met him, all sorts of diagnoses were being mentioned, the main ones being oppositional defiant disorder on the mental health side of things and emotionally disabled on the educational side. Several clues led me to believe, however, that sensory processing disorder was what was really going on.

One of the first tip-offs was a casual, offhanded comment that his father made about wondering why Henry didn't like to be touched. He would wipe off kisses or would move your hand away if you tried to tousle his hair. There were other hints. Though large and exceptionally strong, he was clumsy. He had to sit in chairs that had arms because he was wiggly (which his father and his teachers took to be an indication of ADHD) and would fall right out of the chair onto his rear end. This provided big laughs in restaurants for everyone except Henry.

His father also told me that he ran awkwardly and avoided doing anything that required athletic ability. His refusal to take part in games and sports with other boys had mistakenly been seen as an indication that he was antisocial. The additional fact that he was so impulsively quick to hit had almost sealed the deal on a combined diagnosis of oppositional defiant disorder and ADHD. The treatment plan that had been proposed for him before I met him was that he was to be treated with one medication for his explosive behavior and another to help him focus and make better decisions. None of this sat well with his father, however, testimony to the fact that it is vitally important never to ignore your intuition about your child. As we shall see, following through on such diagnoses would have been a mistake.

Defining Sensory Processing Disorder

What is sensory processing disorder (SPD), previously also known as sensory integration dysfunction? WebMD (www.webmd.com) provides the following explanation:

> Children with sensory integration dysfunction have difficulty processing information from the senses (touch, movement, smell, taste, vision, and hearing) and responding normally to that information. These children typically have one or more senses that either over- or underreact to stimulation. Sensory integration dysfunction can cause problems with a child's development and behavior.

According to WebMD, children with SPD might display the following symptoms.

- [The children will] either be in constant motion or fatigue easily or go back and forth between the two
- Withdraw when being touched
- Refuse to eat certain foods because of how the foods feel when chewed
- Oversensitive to odors
- Hypersensitive to certain fabrics and wear only clothes that are soft or that they find pleasing

- Dislike getting his or her hands dirty
- Uncomfortable with some movements, such as swinging, sliding, or going down ramps or other inclines. Your young child may have trouble learning to climb, go down stairs, or ride an escalator.
- Have difficulty calming himself or herself after exercise or after becoming upset
- Jump, swing, and spin excessively
- Appear clumsy, trip easily, or have poor balance
- Have odd posture
- Have difficulty handling small objects such as buttons or snaps
- Overly sensitive to sound. Vacuum cleaners, lawn mowers, hair dryers, leaf blowers, or sirens may upset your child.
- Lack creativity and variety in play. For instance, your child may play with the same toys in the same manner over and over.

Carol Stock Kranowitz, in her popular book *The Out-of-Sync Child,* indicates that SPD is caused by the inability of a child's neurological system to process and use sensory information efficiently. Kranowitz breaks SPD down into various categories. The most common category is *sensory modulation problems.* Children with these problems may be overresponsive to touch, sometimes responding with a fight-or-flight response to even a light touch. This was Henry's main symptom. Kranowitz also points out that some children in this category are underresponsive to touch (hardly noticing touch, pressure, or texture), and others seek high levels of sensory input. The seekers might like wallowing in mud, rummaging in bins of toys purposelessly, chewing on clothing, bumping into others on purpose, or spinning round and round.

Such symptoms help explain why these children are frequently misdiagnosed as having ADHD.

The second category that Kranowitz describes is *sensory discrimination problems.* Children with these problems have difficulty handling objects, tools, or utensils and may have trouble feeling how hot or cold an object is. They may not realize that they are falling, may be "klutzy," and may have difficulty knowing how much force to use when writing or gripping objects. They may have difficulty understanding likenesses and differences in pictures and written words, reading facial expressions, and lining up columns when adding numbers. They also may have poor auditory discrimination, which can cause trouble picking up what is being said when there is distracting background noise. In addition, they may have difficulty differentiating tastes, such as sweet versus sour.

Kranowitz's third category is *sensory-based motor problems.* Children with these problems may have weak muscle tone, which makes it difficult to grasp or hold anything or to maintain a bodily position. They may have marked difficulties with balance and coordination.

Additionally, when a child's moods and emotions vary to the point that they appear to be out of control, it may prove useful to consider sensory processing problems. Difficulties with sensory input can lead to overarousal or underarousal, which in turn can lead to mood and behavior problems.

If your child is overreactive to touch or displays any of the other symptoms noted above, you need to consider the possibility of sensory processing issues. While the disorder is relatively unknown to the general public, estimates of its prevalence among incoming kindergartners range roughly from 5 to 13 percent, not exactly an inconsequential number.

Treatment Options

You may have to be the one who suggests SPD to your child's doctor, because it remains relatively unknown in mainstream medicine. Its symptoms are easily confused with other issues, and you can see from Henry's case how easy it is for a child to get misdiagnosed.

When you meet with your child's doctor, request a referral to an occupational therapist who specializes in pediatrics. If there are no pediatric occupational therapists available in your area, ask to speak with an occupational therapist who has some background and knowledge in SPD. If no one suitable is available, you will be forced to travel. Most teaching hospitals have pediatric occupational therapists on staff, and many occupational therapy departments at large universities have clinics that are open to the public. The occupational therapist will apprise you and your child's doctor of the need for treatment and will develop a set of treatment procedures.

If it turns out that your child's explosive behavior is due to sensory processing issues, you cannot treat him with the same methods that you would use to treat other causes of explosive behavior. If you use the wrong method, you will get nowhere fast and end up frustrating your child and yourself immensely.

Treatment options vary widely, and procedures are individualized to fit the needs of each child. There is no "five-step" treatment program for SPD. In general, treatment techniques revolve around helping the child accept and deal with sensory input in a more adaptive manner. One child I know who was exceptionally sensitive to anything that came into contact with his bare feet was treated by having him step into boxes that contained rice or marbles. The point was to help him get used to various textures and sensations so that they did not overwhelm him and send him into a panic or rage.

Children who are overreactive to touch may be taught through practice to remain calm while being stroked or massaged, the object being to get the central nervous system used to such stimulation. Children with poor muscle tone or poor balance may do various types of exercises to help them overcome these deficits. Children who shrink from certain textures, smells, or tastes can be exposed to new textures, smells, or tastes in order to help them become less defensive to these inputs.

In Henry's case, treatment went in two directions. First, I referred him to a pediatric occupational therapist who worked with him on his "tactile defensiveness," using a number of methods that taught him not to overrespond to touch, pressure, texture, unexpected motion, and so on.

Second, I came up with a desensitization procedure that I referred to as "bump training," which I have since used successfully with many children—almost all of them boys—who overreact to or shrink away from the typical bumping and banging that is so much a part of the "guy world." In Henry's case, this is how it worked. I asked Henry's father to give Henry a light bump, using his forearm, every time he walked past Henry. This was to be done with a great deal of humor—his dad was to make crashing and exploding sounds every time he did it. Henry was invited to do the same to his dad, so that he could learn how strong a bump should be in order to be seen as normal and fun, and how much was too much, possibly hurtful to others.

My goal was to help Henry get to the point where being bumped would register in his mind as "no big deal," as opposed to "I'm being attacked." I had him practice saying those very words to himself when his dad bumped him: "No big deal. I'm not being attacked." Of course, none of this was done to purposely irritate Henry, although it certainly did at first. "You're doing it on purpose," he would shout at his dad, "just like they do at school." His dad would respond that yes, he was indeed doing it on purpose, although the kids at school were not. He further explained that the reason he was doing it was to show Henry that while it might be irritating to get bumped, it was not an assault, could not hurt him, and was something he had to learn to deal with without exploding.

A couple of other techniques also were useful with Henry. I taught him to politely ask others to try not to bump into him instead of lashing out. I did role plays and simulations with him in my office and had his father do the same at home. He did not enjoy these simulations, because doing them meant that he had to get bumped. He did learn the technique, however, and his father rewarded his hard work by taking him on various "boys' nights out," at which time Henry could choose an activity to do or a restaurant to go to. His teacher also agreed to allow him to stand at the end of the line instead of in the middle if he was having a particularly hard day. However, we did not allow him to use SPD to avoid standing in line at all.

I asked Henry's father to make sure that Henry was consistently involved in group-based activities, such as scouting and school clubs, so that he could learn to deal with his peers in an enjoyable, cooperative way. His balance issues precluded some sports, but I did not think that swimming was out of the question, nor were hiking, fishing, and camping.

I cannot tell you that Henry ever came to enjoy the bump training. I suspect that he will grow up to be an overly serious young man in comparison to his peers, a classic example of how personality and other sensitivities can interact to profoundly affect someone's lifestyle. Much to his credit, he did cease attacking his peers, and talk of medications and placing him in a self-contained special education room for children with emotional disabilities faded away.

By contrast, many of the other boys I work with who have sensory modulation difficulties seem almost set free from their fears of being hurt by using bump training and can't wait to bump and bang with me as we walk down the hallway to my office. When she sees this, my office manager has learned to just shake her head and mutter dark things to herself about Y chromosomes and the nature of men and boys.

12

I'M TIRED!

*

FOR SOME CHILDREN, the most explosion-prone part of the day is first thing in the morning. They wake up like grizzly bears coming out of hibernation – grumpy, touchy, and best left alone. For other children, the battle comes at bedtime. And for still others, both times of the day are rough.

I always ask about sleep patterns when I first meet with an explosive child's parents, because of the known connections between sleep, mood, and behavior. Sometimes it comes out that the child has great difficulty getting to sleep or staying asleep, or that he does not regularly sleep in his or her own bed. Often I hear that the child is afraid to sleep alone, snores loudly enough to wake up the rest of the family, or struggles with bed-wetting. And then there are those children who simply refuse to go to bed at a reasonable hour and insist over and over that they are not sleepy, even though waking them up the next morning is like poking at that bear I mentioned above.

According to the National Sleep Foundation, about 70 percent of children under the age of eleven experience some type of sleep problem, yet many parents and doctors fail to consider sleep seriously enough in explaining children's behavioral problems. Perhaps it is because children usually don't verbalize that they are feeling unrefreshed after sleep and are thus cranky and irritable. They can't make the connection between poor sleep and impulsivity, bad decision making, or difficulty controlling their emotions. To further complicate the situation, parents frequently don't know how to read the signs that a child is sleep deprived.

University of Michigan sleep researcher Ronald Chervin, who has examined the relationship between sleep and children's behavior, says that children who are tired often don't appear tired. Instead of the more quiet and subdued appearance that adults tend to display when sleep deprived, children actually become *more* active. In an effort to stay awake, especially at school, these children will struggle to create an environment that is stimulating enough to keep them awake. It is possible, therefore, that some children who receive behavioral and ADHD diagnoses are in reality just very tired little tots struggling to stay awake!

Imagine for a moment what it must feel like to a child who gets only five or six hours of real sleep each night, when she should be getting ten. She must get up at 6:30 A.M., rush around to get dressed, grab something to eat, gather up her books and backpack, and catch the bus to school, and then immediately begin focusing on difficult material that is being presented by her teacher, despite the overwhelming urge to simply close her eyes. Factor in the boy who sits behind her constantly poking her in the back with a pencil or making noises to try to bug her, and you can see that it is enough to make anyone explosive. And then this same child must take the bus home, go to soccer practice or ballet or gymnastics, interact with her siblings, eat dinner, and do her homework. Many of these children wait until they are safe at home to explode, but some melt down at school as well.

Signs of Sleep Problems

Numerous physical and emotional factors can be related to sleep problems, and some are related to age as well. For example, infants tend to have difficulty sleeping through the night, while

Amount of Sleep Needed by Children

So how much sleep does your child need? The National Sleep Foundation recommends the following number of hours each night. Keep in mind that two- to three-year-olds may still need daily naps in addition to their evening sleep.

Infants	14–15 hrs.
Toddlers (ages 1.5–3)	12–14 hrs.
Preschoolers (ages 3–5)	11–13 hrs.
Elementary school children (ages 6–10)	10–11 hrs.
Middle school children (ages 11–13)	9–10 hrs.

school-age children have problems with nightmares, sleepwalking, bed-wetting, and snoring. If your child has one or more of the following problems several times per week, consider that sleep problems may be contributing to or causing his explosive behavior.

- Consistently falls asleep too early or too late in the evening
- Consistently wakes up too early or too late in the morning
- Wakes you up repeatedly during the night for various reasons
- Snores
- Wets the bed
- Has nightmares and sleep terrors
- Seems to be afraid of going to sleep at night
- Is irritable, hyperactive, or explosive during the day
- Falls asleep during school
- Constantly yawns

Keep in mind that almost every child will have some of these problems from time to time, but if they are recurrent or if your child complains a lot about them, you need to pay attention.

The Importance of Sleep Routines

It is important for parents to try to observe a regular sleep routine and schedule for their children. A regular bedtime is so important, in fact, that the National Sleep Foundation has cited it as the number one tip in promoting good sleep habits. Many parents let their young children talk them into effectively setting their own bedtimes. While it might be fun for the child, a haphazard schedule in which the child goes to bed at 8:00 P.M. one night but stays up watching TV or playing video games until 11:00 P.M. the next night does not promote rest. In addition, some parents allow children to have a TV or gaming system in their rooms—a practice I recommend against because it not only leads to a child developing an isolated lifestyle, but it also leaves him or her free to stealthily watch TV or play video games until the wee hours of the morning. Situations like this give children the power to make decisions that they are not mature enough to make. Such situations also greatly increase the potential for disruption of the sleep rhythm cycle, which in turn increases the possibility of explosive behavior or other behavior problems the following day. If your child does not have a regular sleep routine and schedule, you should consider taking the next few weeks to establish one.

What do I mean by a regular routine and schedule? I mean building in some activities that occur each night to help relax your child and give him cues that it is time for sleep, then enforcing that bedtime night after night. This, by the way, does not include TV, and it does not include feverishly doing homework until the bitter end. The themes of late-night television are often not suitable for children and may sometimes be the very cause of nighttime worries. Homework tends to be rather stressful, especially studying for upcoming tests, and is not a good lead-in activity to going to bed.

The stresses on children today are immense. The pressure to get into college seems almost to begin in grade school, with the notion that a child must make the A/B honor roll, be a super athlete, play an instrument, be in scouts, and on and on. While some children thrive under these conditions, others do not. Each child's schedule needs to be managed by rational parents who know the child's limits. This may mean reducing afterschool activities if your child is always dog-tired. It may mean writing a note to the teacher indicating that your child was unable to finish his homework that evening. It may mean reassuring your child that not getting an A on every test is no big deal.

In any event, children need a certain amount of time at the end of each day to do nothing but relax and interact with their families so that, at a set time each night, after a relaxing bath and perhaps a healthy snack, they can put on their pajamas, brush their teeth, crawl into bed, and allow their minds and bodies to rest. Once your child is tucked in, you should leave the room, and the child should be expected to go to sleep. From time to time, you will need to be flexible, as too much rigidity can sap spontaneity and fun, such as when a child has a friend over on the weekend or when the family is doing something extra special in the evening.

If the child is young, a bedtime story or time spent with a parent discussing the day's events in a calm, unhurried manner can be another way of helping him wind down. Some of the parents I work with have found it helpful to lie down next to the child each night and spend the last thirty minutes of the day discussing any worries the child may have. It is amazing what will spill out of a child when he is feeling comfortable, safe, and relaxed. I also encourage parents to discuss the child's interests at this time. You must display what I refer to as a "fascinated ear." Developing a keen interest in what interests your child can help strengthen the bond between you, and this routine can make for a positive end to the day.

Many parents of overly tired and explosive children feel so angry and stressed-out themselves that they are not willing or able to share this kind of closeness with their children. How many times have I heard, "Dr. Riley, I can't wait for the end of the day when she goes to bed. I hate to admit it, but I just can't stand even being around her anymore!" Though understandable, this is a shortsighted approach and one that may only serve to make the child more insecure and explosive. Forcing yourself to lie down at the end of the day to lovingly talk to your child about hopes and dreams, worries and fears, will go a long way toward helping to calm her and get her ready for sleep.

Fears, Worries, Nightmares, and Other Nighttime Awakenings

I have known some children who don't know what the words "worry" and "fear" mean. I have known others who live by those words. Neither scenario is good. For children, fears and worries surface more readily when they are alone in bed in the dark at the end of the day. Some children naturally find positive ways to ignore these fears, such as allowing themselves to drift off into fantasyland, idly thinking about all the fun things that may happen the next day. Other children cope with their nighttime worries in unexpected and sometimes shocking ways.

One ten-year-old girl I saw a number of years ago came in for the first time with a bald patch about the size of a fifty-cent piece on the top of her head. She had begun pulling out hairs, one by one, as she lay in bed trying to get to sleep. This had progressed to pulling out her eyelashes, one by one, as well. Her mother, who was very embarrassed and angry at what her daughter had done, had purchased false eyelashes for her to wear to school, but the girl had developed an allergy to the adhesive and wasn't able to wear them.

It is difficult to understand why some people get positive feelings from pain, but they usually do such things to release the pent-up emotions that they can't get rid of otherwise. As one teenager with a history of cutting her wrists so aptly put it, "Anything feels better than the worries." If you find that your child is dealing with his fears in an expressive manner—pulling out hair, biting fingernails to the quick, picking at the skin until bleeding occurs—this is a sign that he needs professional help.

Help Your Child Fight His Fears

Children who worry often have the most difficulty separating from their parents at bedtime and going to sleep. Many parents relate to me how the child holds on for dear life when the parent bends down to give a good-night kiss. Once alone, the child tosses and turns or lies awake for hours, sometimes calling out for her parents over and over for reassurance. Such children are afraid of the dark and worry about monsters, dying, bullies at school, grades and school performance, and so on. These worries intrude into their dreams in the form of nightmares, sleep talking, or night terrors. When morning comes, they are too tired to get up for school, too tired to eat, cranky, and apt to lose control of themselves at the drop of a hat.

There are some commonsense things you can do to help your child in this regard. If he is afraid of the dark, provide a nightlight or make sure that some light from the hallway gets into his room. If your child is afraid of monsters and people who may break into the house at night, by all means control what he watches on TV and videos. It is shocking how many parents allow their children to watch Chucky movies, for instance, knowing all the while that the child has nightmares about marauding dolls.

A strategy that often works well for children prone to bad dreams involves having the child recount the bad dream aloud to you. Then the two of you can come up with all the reasons why the dream doesn't make sense. For instance, how many news stories have there been involving monsters that sprang out of a closet at night?

I sometimes like to use what I refer to as my "camera theory" with children who are genuinely convinced that ghosts and monsters and aliens are real. I tell them that there are about seventy-five million families in the United States and each family has approximately two cameras in the house. Yet no one has ever been able to take a photograph of a ghost or monster or alien residing in a child's closet or under a child's bed (or anywhere else for that matter).

Another silly but effective approach is for the two of you to make up some new, more pleasant details to flesh out the dream. For instance, I tell kids that when they recount the bad dream, they can take their laser beam eyeballs and shrink the monster or ghost or alien down to the size of a bug, then imagine squishing it. Or they can use their laser beam eyeballs to heat the monster up until it explodes, monster guts and juice flying everywhere!

Train Your Child to Fall Asleep

Helping your child take action against his fears rather than giving in to them is important. Giving in to an anxious child who either wants you to sleep with him or wants to sleep in your bed is not advisable. I have seen little good come of this. What starts out as a one-night desperate attempt to get the child to sleep often ends up being a nightly ritual. Some fifteen- and sixteen-year-olds are still not able to sleep alone. You can imagine the underlying shame these young people ultimately feel. One teenage girl I saw a number of years ago was so desperate not to be alone in her bed that she would drag her beanbag chair into her parents' bedroom and sleep there.

If your child is having difficulty sleeping alone and you must stay in the child's room for a while at bedtime in order to calm her by reading a book, telling a story, or giving a relaxing back rub, by all means do so. But then insist on leaving the room. It will be difficult at first, but eventually your child will learn to leave the worries behind and fall asleep on her own.

If your child falls asleep but wakes up time after time during the night, it is important *not* to get into the habit of going in to physically comfort him. This may cause further sleep problems by teaching him that you must be there in order for him to sleep, or it may essentially program your child to wake up during the night in order to get your closeness and attention. Instead, try going to your child's door periodically to let him hear your voice and know that you have not abandoned him. Then firmly indicate that it is time to go back to sleep and leave. Your child must learn to fall asleep on his own, without you being there to physically rock, hug, or comfort him.

In his excellent book *Solve Your Child's Sleep Problems,* Richard Ferber, director of the Center for Pediatric Sleep Disorders at Children's Hospital Boston, describes in detail his popular method of teaching children to put themselves back to sleep. This method, which has worked well for my patients, goes something like this: If the child is crying out for you in the night, wait five minutes before going to the door. Reassure the child with your voice, but do not go into the room. If the child continues to cry, wait ten minutes before going to the door. Ferber suggests limiting the waiting period to fifteen minutes for the first night you begin implementing this strategy. Each night after that, attempt to increase the waiting period by five minutes. Most children will eventually learn not to expect physical comfort from their parents and will teach themselves to go back to sleep. Consider this an important skill that you are teaching your child, as opposed to feeling guilty about allowing your child to cry.

Use a Reward System

Using a positive reward system as part of a behavior modification plan to help children reach their goals, including their sleep goals, can be effective. One example will serve to illustrate this. Karen was nine and, like many children, was hesitant to go to bed because being alone in her room made her feel vulnerable. She refused to go to sleep unless her mother or father promised that he or she would be up for several hours after she went to bed, basically to guard the house. This was the only thing that would give her enough psychological ease to get into bed and go to sleep.

I put her on a countdown program with a reward. This is how it worked: On the first night of the program, her parents told her that they would be up for 120 minutes after she went to bed. If she was able to stay in her bed throughout the night, in the morning she would receive a reward of fifty cents, something she valued highly because there was "girl stuff" that she wanted to be able to buy on her own. On the second night, her parents were to be up for 110 minutes, with another fifty-cent reward in the morning for a successful night's sleep. The interval would decrease by 10 minutes nightly, with the reward staying the same. We built in a mechanism to begin to adjust the program because we knew that as the interval between Karen going to bed and her parents going to bed shortened, her anxiety level might rise. For example, once we got down to 40 minutes, the interval could change by as little as 2 minutes a night, from 40 to 38, then from 38 to 36, and so on. The theory behind this was that as she continued to be exposed to briefer and briefer time periods between her bedtime and her parent's bedtime, she would gain the comfort and confidence to go to sleep.

I also added a kicker to the deal. I told her that I was aware that her biggest fear was having to go to bed after her mother went to bed. (Like many girls her age, she was much more sensitive to what her mother was doing than what her father was doing.) The kicker I added was that on occasion, after Karen had been reducing her intervals and was feeling successful and brave, her mother would actually go to bed 15 minutes *earlier* than Karen. If Karen dealt with this peacefully and then went to bed and stayed in her own bed through the night, she would get a five-dollar reward the next morning, a huge sum in her eyes. I told Karen and her parents that if she did not make it peacefully through the night, it was OK and she would be given this opportunity again.

As it turned out, it took only a few nights of decreasing the interval by 10 minutes before Karen wanted to try earning the five-dollar reward. She got through the night and received her money the next day. Did it provide a miracle cure? No, it did not—few things do. But Karen did feel quite proud that she had faced her fears and became much more optimistic about reaching her goal. If you think all the way back to the material in chapter 2 on how both talk and actual exposure to the feared situation are key to the brain becoming calm, you can see why this program worked for Karen. We talked it out, but we also gave her the opportunity to face her fears. She continued to work her program until she was able, several months down the road, to go to bed on her own without any difficulty.

Dramatic Sleep Disturbances

Night terrors and sleep talking, sleepwalking, and thrashing about in bed are some of the more dramatic sleep disturbances. These tend to occur during partial awakenings from a deep, nondreaming sleep and do not necessarily mean that your child has any deep-seated emotional problems that you need to be concerned about. It may simply be that your child's sleep rhythms are still maturing. He may need some comforting from you after these incidents, though many children simply go right back to sleep. As your child matures, these issues may very well go away.

When frequent night terrors and sleepwalking continue past the age of six and into adolescence, psychological factors may be involved. Children who have these symptoms are almost always worried about something, such as not doing well enough in school or not being popular enough, pretty enough, or tough enough. They may be worried when they hear parents arguing too much, or when someone in the family is ill. When these children do not voice their fears and feelings to someone, their worries often get expressed as sleep disturbances.

Sleep talking is just that: talking while sleeping. Sleepwalking occurs when a child spontaneously gets up and calmly begins walking around without being aware of what she is doing. Night terrors occur when a child suddenly sits up in bed and cries out or even screams frantically. The child also may run about the room as if in a panic. When you try to speak to the child, she may answer, but not in a logical sense.

Eight-year-old John's parents brought him in to see me because of his night terrors. He would wake up suddenly and begin screaming at the top of his lungs. Sometimes his parents would find him standing on his bed, arms outstretched, turning around in circles. At other times, he would run down the upstairs hallway, with his parents chasing him so that he would not tumble down the stairs. Although these episodes can be frightening to parents, they are much more common than you might think and will likely go away as the child matures physically and emotionally. It is important that parents let the child know that he is not "crazy" because he sleep talks, sleepwalks, or has night terrors. Parents should take these sleep issues as helpful clues that the child may have some worries and stresses that he needs help with. If your child continues to feel a great deal of stress that disrupts his sleep on a weekly basis, you may need to seek the help of his pediatrician or a child psychologist.

Snoring, Breathing Problems, and Sleep Apnea

One of the nicest, most mild-mannered young men I have ever worked with struggled with undiagnosed sleep apnea, one form of what is known as sleep-disordered breathing (SDB). Sleep apnea is a condition in which a person actually stops breathing momentarily, over and over again, during the night. The brain jolts the body to breathe once it registers that the person is not getting sufficient oxygen, which moves him or her out of sleep momentarily. The person breathes, then returns to sleep, only to go through the cycle again, over and over. Literally, the person wakes up hundreds of times each night, then falls back to sleep, although he or she rarely reaches the deep stages of sleep that leave him or her rested. Little wonder that the diminished level of oxygen in the person's blood and the lack of restful sleep leave him or her fried and explosive the next morning.

The thirteen-year-old boy who came to see me would be so uncontrollably tired that he would fall asleep during class and begin snoring, which of course made him the laughingstock of the class. To make matters worse, his teacher was always sharply prompting him to "wake up" in front of his classmates. He began responding with aggressive behavior, kicking things or turning his desk over and walking out of class in anger and frustration. He once told me during a session, "It makes me feel like killing somebody. It really does." He punched one fist into another as he talked. "All I want to do is just close my eyes and take a little nap. Just a little nap during school would help so much. Sometimes I ask if I can go to the nurse's office. I say I'm sick just so I can go lie on the bed and take a nap." Thankfully for this boy, his apnea was caused by his enlarged tonsils. Having them removed brought a rapid halt to the apnea and thus to his explosive behavior. He is a good example of how a disturbed sleep pattern can profoundly impact the behavior of a child who otherwise would be doing quite well in the world.

According to the National Institutes of Health, more than 10 percent of young children have a snoring problem, which is the mildest form of SDB. Snoring can be caused by nasal congestion or enlarged tonsils or adenoids. Some children who snore may also have sleep apnea, which I discussed earlier. African American children are twice as likely as Caucasian children to develop SDB, and children who are overweight stand a greater chance of developing this disorder than normal weight children.

A number of important studies have shown a direct link between SDB and both behavioral problems and low performance on standardized tests. A 2006 study cited in *Pediatrics* indicates that children with SDB who have surgery to remove their tonsils are likely to behave and sleep better one year later. In fact, about half of the children who had been diagnosed with ADHD before tonsil surgery no longer met the criteria for this diagnosis one year later. The researchers indicated that these results do not necessarily show cause and effect and that a tonsillectomy cannot be considered a "cure" for ADHD. However, the potential for beneficial effects for sleep-deprived and ADHD children is certainly worth noting.

Keep in mind that children who have ADHD also tend to be more impulsive and explosive, underscoring the point that poor sleep as a result of SDB can certainly result in explosive behavior. If you suspect that your child's explosive behavior may be the result of SDB, you should consult your pediatrician for help in this area.

Bed-wetting

Bed-wetting can interfere with a child's sleep, and it is important to know how to handle it properly, not only in regard to eliminating potential explosive behavior issues but also in regard to the child's self-concept issues. Most studies show that regular bedwetting occurs in approximately 40 percent of four-year-olds, 15 percent of five-year-olds, and 5 percent of ten-year-olds. Children with bed-wetting issues and their parents all seem relieved when they hear these statistics, because they are sure that they are the only ones who are dealing with this problem.

Why do some children struggle with bed-wetting while others do not? An immature nervous system, a small bladder capacity, an increased production of urine during the night, or an infection or neurological condition (though these are accompanied by other daytime symptoms, such as painful urination, blood in the urine, inability to urinate, or strong urges to urinate) may be to blame. Other possible causes are food sensitivities, stress, or anxiety. Finally, heredity is a strong contributing factor. If one parent was a late bed wetter, the child has a much stronger chance of frequent bed-wetting over the age of five.

Given all of this, it is important that parents let their children know that bed-wetting is not their fault and that in time their bodies will adjust. Parents also must summon up the patience that is required to help a child through this problem, because bed-wetting does not just take a toll on the sleep cycle of the child; it affects the sleep of the parents as well, especially if the accidents are happening every night. Many times the child will wake up in a soaking-wet bed and call out to the parents for help. This usually means that one of the parents must get up from a deep sleep, change the child's bedding and clothes, in some cases comfort and reassure the child, and do this all without sounding punishing or angry. No easy task! It is, however, vitally important that both parents support each other during this time by taking turns getting up during the night and by giving each other pep talks about the importance of not being too critical of the child.

Several strategies for dealing with bed-wetting may be useful.

- Make sure that you have ruled out any neurological problems that may affect the urinary tract. Your child's pediatrician can help here.
- Explain to your child how the bladder works. Tell her that the bladder is like an expandable balloon with a muscle at the end that can be squeezed shut to keep the urine from coming out. Sometimes kids sleep so soundly that their brains stop reminding the muscle to squeeze itself shut. As they grow older, this mechanism happens on its own. This explanation may help to take the mystery, fear, and blame away from your child.
- Have your child avoid drinking large amounts of fluids after 6:00 P.M., though remember that restricting fluids too much can cause dehydration.
- Make sure that your child empties her bladder completely before bedtime. Some children are in a rush to get to bed and only half-empty their bladders.

- Try waking your child up before you go to bed or at certain intervals during the night to allow her to urinate.
- If your child is allergic or sensitive to a particular food, such as milk, she may have more trouble with enuresis. (See chapter 3 for more on this issue.) By eliminating the offending food, you may solve the bed-wetting problem as well as a host of other problems.
- You have heard me talk about the big guy/little guy approach earlier in this book. This approach is based on the idea that children have the intrinsic desire to be considered "big." To this effect, if a child is given "big guy" or "big girl" responsibilities around the house, such as vacuuming his room or setting the table for dinner, he will begin to internalize "bigness" to include acting responsibly in other aspects of his life as well. In this vein, if your child is age six or older and has an accident in bed, she should act "big" by attempting to change into dry pajamas and may even be able to help put fresh sheets on the bed. It is very important not to make this seem like a punishment, but rather a way to help the child think of herself in a positive manner.
- Consider medication. For older children or children who do not respond to other strategies, medication may be the answer. Check with your child's pediatrician for more information on this.

Sleep Problems and Other Issues

I must finally note that sleep problems seem to coexist so frequently with other disorders that whenever you realize that your child has a sleep issue, you should also be on the lookout for attention issues, cognitive problems, oppositional behavior, social problems, depression, anxiety, and, of course, explosive behavior. It is clearly important to address any existing weight issues not only because of the potential long-term health problems associated with being overweight, but also because weight loss can improve SDB. A last area of concern is the connection between sleep-related problems and family functioning. While it may not appear that family tensions are having an obvious impact on a child, sometimes that stress is expressed as a sleep problem. If this is the case in your family, it would be wise to seek family counseling or marital counseling.

13

OCKHAM'S RAZOR

A Guiding Principle for Decreasing Explosions

YOU MAY BE FAMILIAR with Ockham's razor, a theory of parsimony attributed to the fourteenth-century monk William of Ockham. The theory states that in any given situation, the simplest solution is likely the best solution. This serves as an excellent guiding principle in your work with an explosive child. You should start with the simplest solutions in hopes that they may work with your child and only move to more complex solutions as needed. I have seen many, many children over the years who have ceased blowing up when their parents and teachers began to give them the type of systematic verbal feedback that I discussed in the section on the big kid program in chapter 2. Often there is no need to seek more complex forms of counseling and treatment.

I run into parents on a daily basis who assume that they have delivered enough verbal praise if they occasionally say something positive to their children about their behavior. When I talk about praise-based interventions, their response is "I've done that. It doesn't work." However, it is unlikely that they have tried it on as frequent and consistent a basis as I intend. While it is true that there is no magic bullet, sometimes *consistently* praising a child for her appropriate behavior and reminding her in an upbeat and *consistent* manner that she needs to improve when she is about to go off the beam will produce remarkable results. In particular, parents who have been yellers and screamers and who have concentrated only on their children's mistakes will have to devote a lengthy period of time (weeks at least, and probably months) to using this strategy in order to prove to their children that they have made their own changes and are no longer going to flip out as a response to their kids' behavior. Remember, the vast majority of young children aspire to being big and will try their best to live up to this when given feedback and praise. This type of intervention takes only seconds to deliver ("Hey, I really like the way you acted on the playground today! Total big kid zone!") but can be an incredibly powerful balm to a child's soul. Verbal praise for older kids about the appropriateness and maturity of their behavior is similarly easy to deliver.

If the simplest solution—verbal praise—does not work for your young child, by all means combine it with physical praise (hugs and high-fives) and public praise (rounds of applause at the dinner table for having had a great day, rounds of applause from the child's classmates for having had a successful morning or afternoon, naming the child line leader as a reward for successful behavior, hanging up signs on the refrigerator for a great week at school).

If physical praise and public praise do not work, move to intensified reinforcement strategies. Some of the children I work with do well using a program in which they get a small reward nightly for having had a successful day (a Popsicle, video game time, a later bedtime, or access to a special toy or object). If the child maintains her behavior from Monday through Friday, she also gets a much more substantial reward on the weekend, such as having a friend over to spend the night, going out for a movie or a pizza, going fishing, going on a long bike ride, or having a play date at a special kids' gym. The beauty of this program is that the child gets a daily reinforcer—working for something that is a week away is too abstract for most young children—and if she maintains her effort all week, the reward is even larger. If she fails at some point during the week, she is not placed in the sad position of losing everything. She can still work to get the small daily reward. Each week starts anew on Monday morning and brings the hope of gaining that big prize on the weekend.

If you move through the praise and reinforcement strategies to no avail, it does not mean that these methods are not useful. It does mean that you will clearly have to intensify your effort to determine which of the various hidden causes of explosive behavior we have examined in this book are most likely to have a grip on your child's life. As you become aware of the cause, the treatment also makes itself evident. For example, children who explode repeatedly because they get bumped into or because someone brushes against them, or those who display other indications of sensory processing disorder such as aversions to certain clothing textures or food textures, should be evaluated by a pediatric occupational therapist, who can develop a treatment plan that will help them with their bodily sensitivities.

Likewise, if it becomes apparent that there is a food connection to your child's explosions and cranky behavior, remove the offending food(s) from her diet. Access to this food for other members of the family will have to be strictly controlled so that the allergic child cannot sneak it. This will never be easy, but it will be necessary.

Kids who explode because of unexpected events or transitions will have to be exposed to them at a high level so that they become desensitized to them. Anxious kids should be engaged in talk therapy to find what they are using as proof that things are bound to turn out badly.

Depressed kids, like anxious kids, will benefit from talking to someone trained in cognitive behavior therapy, particularly if they talk about the negative beliefs that they harbor about themselves and their lives. But it is equally important to get them out into the world, into the mix of people and places and things, so that they can learn how to experience fun and enjoyment. Be prepared for the child to complain that nothing will help her, and in the beginning she will tell you that she does not enjoy any of the things you are having her do. This is her depression speaking, and it's your job to help her regain her sense of hope for the future.

Get used to going to meetings and strategy sessions with teachers if you have a child who has a learning disability. Get used to lobbying your child's school to develop a curriculum for him that will take advantage of his strengths and help strengthen his weaknesses. Set up tutoring sessions with teachers or private tutors, and be ready to fight with your child about going to these sessions.

As you intensify the search for what is causing your child's explosions, you may find that there is more than one issue at play, each of which can cause explosive behavior. The term for this is "comorbidity." An example of this is a child who cannot concentrate, is depressed, and has poor social skills.

Co-occurrence of symptoms is surprisingly common. Up to a third of children with OCD also have ADHD; children with OCD also commonly suffer from anxiety, oppositional behavior, or depression; the overlap between ADHD and depression, or ADHD and oppositional behavior, can be as high as 56 percent; and children with learning disabilities display emotional and behavioral problems up to four times more often than children without learning disabilities. Even allergy sufferers, if you recall, are known to suffer from sharply increased rates of learning, behavioral, and emotional problems compared to their peers without allergies.

Do not lose heart! While you might intuitively believe that children carrying such a heavy load of emotional issues might prove impossible to treat, you should be aware of an intriguing study by Yale University researchers Alan Kazdin and Moira Whitley, which was designed to test what is known as the complexity hypothesis. This hypothesis states that the more complex a case is, as in children having multiple diagnosable disorders, the greater the chances that the child will not respond to treatments that have been shown to work in less complex cases. The study focused on 183 children who were referred for disruptive behavior. Over 78 percent of the participants whose primary diagnosis was oppositional defiant disorder met the criteria for more than one disorder, with some subjects meeting the criteria for as many as five additional disorders, including depression, ADHD, separation anxiety, overanxious disorder, and adjustment disorder. The study found that children with more than one disorder actually showed greater change by the end of counseling than children with a single disorder.

The Kazdin and Whitley study is important for several reasons. First, their findings remind us to maintain our optimism in the face of a complex set of symptoms. Sometimes, if we are persistent and lucky, we put our finger on a linchpin issue. Getting help with that one issue makes all of the child's symptoms come crashing down like a house of cards, a lesson in how everything is interconnected.

A wonderful example of this was another boy (age ten) who was referred to me because he was explosive at home and complained of feeling tired all day at school. He snored like a freight train at night and got lots of ribbing about it. I asked his parents to bring up his sleep issues with his pediatrician and to consider having a sleep study done. The pediatrician took one look down the boy's throat and, according to his mother, said, "My God, he can't breathe!" He was referred to an ear, nose, and throat specialist and had his tonsils and adenoids removed. This resulted in his getting more restful sleep, which resolved his irritability and explosive behavior and helped him stay awake at school. His parents thanked me for bringing up the issue of a sleep study because it had led them back to his pediatrician. But they were also happily emphatic that he no longer needed my help.

It is more common than you might imagine to find such linchpin issues. At the same time, there are many cases in which a child displays multiple symptoms and the best we can do is work on each issue systematically, one at a time. Where do we start? Again, ask yourself what is the *main* thing that you know or suspect or have observed about your child. Which symptom seems to have the most strength, the most push? In such situations, we continue to tap away at the symptoms, using treatment techniques that are specifically designed to help with that symptom.

Will following my suggestions always make your child happy? Of course not. But I have seen remarkable transformations in the explosive children I work with when parents and therapists are persistent. Will you have similar success with your child or the children you work with professionally? There is absolutely nothing to make me think that you won't, because I have seen the methods that I've covered in this book give families and children rapid relief over the many years that I have been using them. I have come to believe that all exploding children are capable of a big turnaround once we identify the underlying causes of their explosions.

14

FINAL THOUGHTS ON LIVING AND WORKING WITH EXPLOSIVE CHILDREN

*

THE MAIN THING an explosive child needs from you is for you not to be an explosive adult. Whether your child or the children you work with professionally explode due to road map issues or depressed mood or any other reason, you must remember that none of them is exploding on purpose. Even the ones who make the most conscious effort to be bad actors, the oppositional children, can't be said to be fully in control of themselves. We all know that they are operating out of a fantasy and are not in touch with reality when it comes to thinking clearly about the disparity in rights, power, and privileges between them and the adults. The one thing that you can be sure of is that once a child explodes, he is completely lost and needs someone — most likely you — to guide him back to safety.

There is a particular attitude that you must adopt to intervene successfully in the lives of explosive children, and I have hinted at it earlier. I refer to it as "bemused detachment." The "bemused" part is there to remind you that children who explode need to be dealt with kindly and gently, and the only way you can pull this off is to be aware of the humor that is implicit in their attempt to defeat you. Your three-foot-tall child has to be mighty optimistic to take you on, and if you pause for just a moment to ask yourself what real chance she has of defeating you, you can't help but chuckle. As I have said hundreds of times to worn-out parents, "You own everything. All your child owns is his attitude." Such a disparity of power leaves your child with no chance, none whatsoever, of taking you on successfully, at least not as long as you control yourself and maintain the viewpoint that your child will never be your coequal. Still, your child will try to defeat you, something that should be part of the official definition of the word "childhood."

As for the "detachment" part, any explosive child will do his best to get you to engage in a battle. When you engage with an out-of-control child by losing control of yourself or get on the maturity elevator and descend to his level, it is akin to getting down in the swamp with an alligator. You'd best anticipate the beating you are about to take if you make this trip, because a child who is out of control does not play fair. He will bait you by hurling insults at you ("You stupid head!") or by going straight for your heart ("You're a bad, bad momma!"). He might kick you or spit at you or take a poke at you. The moment that you take this personally and your emotions begin to direct your actions, your authority as parent and head of the family begins to slip away. As a very wise mother told me, once you get down to his level and yell and scream and argue and threaten, you will ultimately end up apologizing to him for hurting his feelings, and you will feel like a really rotten human being.

How will you now judge that child you see melting down at the grocery store, the one I talked about at the beginning of chapter 1? Will you still be tempted to think of him as a brat? Or will your mind begin to spin with hypotheses about what might be the real causes of his explosion, as well as the possible solutions? Obviously, I hope that your mind begins to spin at least a little, as that will indicate that you can no longer look at exploding children in simple terms. Hopefully, in an odd sort of way, their explosions will remind you to think about the infinite variety of behaviors and emotions that are part of the human experience and about how we must look at each child as the true individual that he or she is. Anything less, and we fail.

NOTES

1. I AM NOT A BRAT, JUST A CHILD WHO NEEDS HELP

Temperament, particularly in males, can sometimes forecast the direction a person will take with his life. If you are interested in life-span research, consider this important study by Avshalom Caspi and Glen Elder: "Moving Against the World: Life-Course Patterns of Explosive Children," *Developmental Psychology* 23 (1987): 308–13.

2. CHANGES AND TRANSITIONS MAKE ME EXPLODE

Developmental psychologists are interested in how children learn to regulate their own behavior in various settings. Susan Calkins and Nathan Fox examined this issue, particularly in regard to social withdrawal and aggression, in "Self-Regulatory Processes in Early Personality Development: A Multilevel Approach to the Study of Childhood Social Withdrawal and Aggression," *Development and Psychopathology* 14 (2002): 477–98.

Two of the lead researchers in the study of child development and temperament are Jerome Kagan and Nancy Snidman at Harvard University. They are particularly interested in the brain's reaction to novel stimuli and how this influences behavior. They examined this in their article "The Physiology and Psychology of Behavioral Inhibition in Children," *Child Development* 58 (1987): 1459–73. It also turns out that other aspects of temperament, such as the ability to self-regulate, have some predictive power regarding child-parent relationship problems. Georgia Degangi and colleagues reported on this in "Prediction of Childhood Problems at

Three Years in Children Experiencing Disorders of Regulation During Infancy," *Infant Mental Health Journal* 21 (2000): 156–75.

While the interaction between the brain and the environment is known to have a strong impact on behavior, it is important to continue to examine environmental variables, such as parental hostility and rejection, on a child's personality. Kerry Bolger and Charlotte Patterson did this in their article "Pathways from Child Maltreatment to Internalizing Problems: Perceptions of Control as Mediators and Moderators," *Development and Psychopathology* 13 (2001): 913–40. However, the influence of parents on childhood behavior sometimes yields surprising results, particularly when it comes to parents who are intrusive. Nathan Fox and colleagues touched on this in "Behavioral Inhibition: Linking Biology and Behavior Within a Developmental Framework," *Annual Review of Psychology* 56 (2005): 235–62. This article also explores the important links between behavioral inhibition, behavioral disinhibition, and behavior.

Shulamith Kreitler and Hans Kreitler examined how the complexity of a child's thinking develops with age. In particular, they were interested in a child's ability to anticipate outcomes, an important aspect of self-control. See "Development of Probability Thinking in Children 5 to 12 Years Old," *Cognitive Development* 1 (1986): 365–90.

Another important article for those interested in behavior control is one by Roger Katz of the University of Utah. Katz discusses the important point that failing to provide consequences for a child is likely to make her behavior worse. See "Interactions Between the Facilitative and Inhibitory Effects of a Punishing Stimulus in the Control of Children's Hitting Behavior," *Child Development* 42 (1971): 1433–46.

Aggressive children have been found to have a set of thoughts and beliefs that they turn to routinely to get them through conflict situations. These thoughts and beliefs, referred to as "scripts," tend to lead them to aggressive solutions. See Paul Boxer et al., "Developmental Issues in School-Based Aggression Prevention from a Social-Cognitive Perspective," *Journal of Primary Prevention* 1 (2005): 383–400.

One of the most often cited references in behavioral science is Joseph Wolpe's *Psychotherapy by Reciprocal Inhibition* (Stanford, CA: Stanford University Press, 1958). Additionally, Phillip Kendall and colleagues discuss the part that exposure therapy plays in cognitive behavior therapy (CBT) in their article "Considering CBT with Anxious Youth? Think Exposure," *Cognitive and Behavioral Practice* 12 (2005): 36–150. While there is no consensus as to how exposure therapy works, Professor Rudi De Raedt discusses how areas of the brain communicate with one another to create emotional changes following exposure therapy. See "Does Neuroscience Hold Promise for the Further Development of Behavior Therapy? The Case of Emotional Change After Exposure in Anxiety and Depression," *Scandinavian Journal of Psychology* 47 (2006): 225–36.

For a brief explanation of how visualizing can be used as a counterconditioning procedure when exposure therapy fails to work in an attempt to treat a specific phobia, see Daniel Moran and Richard O'Brien, "Competency Imagery: A Case Study Treating Emetophobia," *Psychological Reports* 96 (2005): 635–36. Additional support for using visual imagery to treat childhood phobias can be found in Nevile King et al., "Usefulness of Emotive Imagery in the Treatment of Childhood Phobias: Clinical Guidelines, Case Examples and Issues," *Counseling Psychology Quarterly* 14 (2001): 95–101.

Kate Keenan and Lauren Wakschlag discuss an important diagnostic issue—how a modified form of the DSM-IV framework can be used to identify preschool children with disruptive behavior. See "Can a Valid Diagnosis of Disruptive Behavior Disorder Be Made in Preschool Children?" *American Journal of Psychiatry* 159 (2002): 351–58.

3. MY ALLERGIES ARE AFFECTING THE WAY I FEEL AND BEHAVE

James Blackman and Matthew Durka's examination of data from the National Survey of Children's Health, conducted in 2003–2004, provides a fascinating look at the behavioral, learning, and emotional issues that affect some asthmatic children. See "Development and Behavioral Comorbidities of Asthma in Children," *Journal of Developmental and Behavioral Pediatrics* 28 (2007): 92–99.

Doris Rapp, *Is This Your Child? Discovering and Treating Unrecognized Allergies in Children and Adults* (New York: William Morrow, 1991), is packed with information on children and food allergies. Dr. Rapp, an allergist, provides an exhaustive list of symptoms and case studies to help parents decide whether their child may have a problem with foods, and she outlines the treatment options available.

The Linus Pauling quote comes from William Philpott and Dwight Kalita, *Brain Allergies: The Psychonutrient and Magnetic Connections*, 2nd ed. (Chicago: Keats Publishing, 2000). This interesting book discusses the dramatic connection between food allergies, vitamin and mineral deficiencies, and the brain. Philpott, an orthomolecular scientist, also provides a thorough and very technical discussion of the food elimination diet and the need for the rotation of foods in the diet.

James Braly and Patrick Holford's *Hidden Food Allergies* (Laguna Beach, CA: Basic Health Publications, 2006) identifies the most common food allergens, discusses the causes of food allergies, provides information on allergy testing, outlines how to do an elimination diet, and discusses how to reverse food allergies. This is an easy-to-follow book that someone who is unfamiliar with the subject can read easily.

4. I DON'T LIKE RULES!

Jerome Kagan and Nancy Snidman, in considering the genetic aspects of childhood behavior, examined the physical and physiological differences between inhibited and uninhibited children. See "Temperamental Contributions to Styles of Reactivity to Discrepancy," in *The Development and Meaning of Psychological Distance*, ed. Rodney Cocking and K. Ann Renninger (Mahwah, NJ: Lawrence Erlbaum, 1993), 81–89.

For a discussion of the differences in how oppositional preschool boys tend to think in comparison to their nonoppositional peers, see Katherine Coy et al., "Social-Cognitive Processes in Preschool Boys With and Without Occupational Defiant Disorder," *Journal of Abnormal Child Psychology* 29 (2001): 107–30. The thought patterns of oppositional children are also extensively examined in my book *The Defiant Child: A Parent's Guide to Oppositional Defiant Disorder* (Dallas: Taylor Trade Publishing, 1997).

5. I'M A WIGGLER AND A DAYDREAMER

Steven Cuffe and colleagues, researchers at the University of South Carolina, examined the National Health Interview Survey results for children ages four to seventeen to determine the prevalence of ADHD symptoms, as well as the other symptoms that seem to accompany it frequently. See "Prevalence and Correlates of ADHD Symptoms in the National Health Interview Survey," *Journal of Attention Disorders* 9 (2005): 392–401. In a similar vein, Mark Sciutto and colleagues discuss the important issue of gender and symptoms in "Effects of Child Gender and Symptom Type on Referrals for ADHD by Elementary School Teachers," *Journal of Emotional and Behavioral Disorders* 12 (2004): 247–53. They concluded that boys are more likely to be referred for special services than girls who displayed the same symptoms. Differences in teacher perception, not actual behavior, may account for the differences in referral rates.

Irwin Waldman and Ian Gizer conducted a review of the studies examining ADHD and the various candidate genes related to neurotransmitter production. See "The Genetics of Attention Deficit Hyperactivity Disorder," *Clinical Psychology Review* 26 (2006): 396–432. Larry Seidman and colleagues, also interested in the differences between children with ADHD and children without it, used brain imaging to search for abnormalities in the frontal area of the brain. They found evidence that brain abnormalities may be implicated in ADHD. See "Structural Brain Imaging of Attention-Deficit Hyperactivity Disorder," *Biological Psychiatry* 57 (2005): 1263–72.

Dave Daley, psychology professor at the University of Wales, reviewed the current research on ADHD to provide a synopsis that clinicians may use to help parents understand the complexities of ADHD. See "Attention Deficit Hyperactivity Disorder: A Review of the Essential Facts," *Child: Care, Health and Development* 32 (2006): 193–204. The differences in IQ between children with ADHD and those without it are trivial. Rather, the major contributing factor to ADHD seems to be impaired executive functioning. For a discussion of this, see Sabrina Schuck and Francis Crinella, "Why Children with ADHD Do Not Have Low IQs," *Journal of Learning Disabilities* 38 (2005): 262–80.

J. M. Halperin and colleagues studied the noradrenergic mechanisms at work in children with ADHD, noting that stimulant medications remain the frontline treatment of choice. See "Noradrenergic Mechanisms in ADHD Children with and Without Reading Disabilities: A Replication and Extension," *Journal of the American Academy of Child and Adolescent Psychiatry* 36 (1997): 1688–97. However, Edmund Sonuga-Barke and colleagues investigated the effects of training parents in recognizing ADHD symptoms and how to use various behavior management techniques, finding that this improved family functioning. See "Parent-Based Therapies for Preschool Attention Deficit/Hyperactivity Disorder: A Randomized, Controlled Trial with a Community Sample," *Journal of the American Academy of Child and Adolescent Psychiatry* 40 (2001): 402–8.

Anyone who is interested in alternatives to medication should read the interesting studies on self-monitoring, a technique in which a child is trained to monitor and record his own on-task behavior. Such techniques typically use either an audible tone, a clock, or a small desktop device to monitor the child's on-task behavior during instruction. A study by Laura Wolfe and colleagues found evidence that self-monitoring and public posting of performance improved on-task behavior. See "Effects of Self-

Monitoring on the On-Task Behavior and Written Language Performance of Elementary Students with Learning Disabilities," *Journal of Behavioral Education* 10 (2002): 49–73.

Similarly, Tina Dalton and colleagues studied two adolescent males with learning disabilities and ADHD, finding that training in the use of a self-monitoring form improved on-task behavior. See "The Effects of a Self-Management Program in Reducing Off Task Behavior," *Journal of Behavioral Education* 9 (1999): 157–76.

Michael Gordon and colleagues examined the practice of placing a small teacher-controlled monitoring device on a child's desk that indicated how many points were being won for on-task behavior. This research also introduced the issue of response cost, studying the effect of the loss of points for off-task behavior. A clear positive effect was seen, although the improvements in on-task behavior reversed rapidly when the monitoring device was not being used. See "Nonmedical Treatment of ADHD/Hyperactivity: The Attention Training System," *Journal of School Psychology* 29 (1991): 151–59.

6. I CAN'T CONTROL MYSELF AT SCHOOL

Laura Griner Hill and Nicole Werner, researchers at Washington State University, found that the more a child feels attached and affiliated with her school, the less likely it is that she will act in an aggressive manner. This is an important study for school officials interested in decreasing school violence. See "Affiliative Motivation, School Attachment, and Aggression in School," *Psychology in the Schools* 43 (2006): 231–46. Along these same lines, Roger Weissberg and colleagues propose the creation of community-based prevention programs specific to the needs of families and children. See "Prevention That Works for Children and Youth: An Introduction," *American Psychologist* 58 (2003): 425–32.

Children who are picked on and rejected by their peers probably do not feel strong ties to their schools. Research shows clearly that peer rejection influences a child's school performance and attendance in a negative way. See Eric Buhs et al., "Peer Exclusion and Victimization: Processes That Mediate the Relation Between Peer Group Rejection and Children's Classroom Engagement and Achievement?" *Journal of Educational Psychology* 98 (2006): 1–13. There is also evidence that the younger children are, the more their risk for developing emotional and behavioral problems, underscoring the need for a healthy school environment. For a review of child psychiatric disorder relative to age, see Robert Goodman et al., "Child Psychiatric Disorder and Relative Age Within School Year: Cross-Sectional Survey of Large Population Sample," *British Medical Journal* 327 (2003), www.bmj.com/cgi/content/full/327/7413/472.

Carmen Broussard and John Northup examined how to control disruptive behavior in the classroom. They found that it decreased when children were taught not to pay attention to a peer who was engaged in disruptive behavior. See "The Use of Functional Analysis to Develop Peer Interventions for Disruptive Classroom Behavior," *School Psychology Quarterly* 12 (1997): 65–76. Also, Deborah Lowe Vandell and Mary Ann Corasaniti found evidence that peer relationships and overall emotional adjustment among low-income children improved when they attended afterschool programs. The implications of this finding are that well-designed afterschool programs have a positive impact on classroom behavior. See "Variations in Early Childcare: Do They Predict Subsequent Social, Emotional, and Cognitive Differences?" *Early Childhood Research Quarterly* 5 (1990): 555–72.

7. I WORRY ABOUT EVERYTHING

An excellent online source of information related to mental health is the Center for Mental Health Services, sponsored by the Substance Abuse and Mental Health Services Administration division of the U.S. Department of Health and Human Services: mentalhealth.samhsa.gov/cmhs.

For a study of how to modify DSM-IV criteria to identify children between the ages of eighteen months and five years who suffer from social anxiety or generalized anxiety disorder, see Susan Warren et al., "Toddler Anxiety Disorders: A Pilot Study," *Journal of the American Academy of Child and Adolescent Psychiatry* 45 (2006): 859–70.

Thalia Eley and colleagues, at the Institute for Psychiatry at King's College London, found strong genetic links for obsessive-compulsive behavior and genetic influences for other anxiety-related behaviors. See "A Twin Study of Anxiety-Related Behaviours in Pre-School Children," *Journal of Child Psychology and Psychiatry* 44 (2003): 945–60. Sabine Wilhelm and D. F. Tolin reviewed treatment of anxiety disorders and found that both medication and cognitive behavior therapy are viable alternatives when treatment is necessary. See "Challenges in Treating Obsessive-Compulsive Disorder: Introduction," *Journal of Clinical Psychology: In Session* 60 (2004): 1127–32.

Children harbor all sorts of thoughts about themselves and others that have a massive impact on their mood and behavior. Often the key to changing behavior is to help a child change how he thinks about himself and the situations he faces. See my book *The Depressed Child: A Parent's Guide for Rescuing Kids* (Dallas: Taylor Trade Publishing, 2001).

8. MAYBE I'M DEPRESSED

Anyone who works with bipolar children, whether in a diagnostic role or a treatment role, should be aware of the core symptoms of pediatric mania, as discussed by Joan Luby and Andy Belden in "Defining and Validating Bipolar Disorder in the Preschool Period," *Development and Psychopathology* 18 (2006): 971–88.

Arman Danielyan and colleagues report on how difficult it is to properly diagnose childhood bipolar disorder. Additionally, they discuss the nature of the strong affect that bipolar children display, one of their defining characteristics. See "Clinical Characteristics of Bipolar Disorder in Very Young Children," *Journal of Affective Disorders* 97 (2007): 51–59. At the same time, Brendan Rich and colleagues caution that while marked irritability may be an indicator of bipolar disorder, it may also be an indicator of severe mood dysregulation (SMD), a relatively new diagnostic category whose pathophysiology is distinctly different from that of bipolar disorder. See "Different Psychophysiological and Behavioral Responses Elicited by Frustration in Pediatric Bipolar Disorder and Severe Mood Dysregulation," *American Journal of Psychiatry* 164 (2007): 309–17.

R. C. Harrington and colleagues examine the pathway that childhood depression often takes into adulthood. See "Adult Outcomes of Childhood and Adolescent Depression: I. Psychiatric Status," *Archives of General Psychiatry* 47 (1990): 465–73. For an excellent online review of the indications of childhood depression, go to www.webmd.com and enter the search term "childhood depression." Or go to www.webmd.com/anxiety-panic/guide/recognizing-childhood-depression-anxiety?page=3.

Samuel Blumberg and Carroll Izard studied the differences between adult and child forms of depression, particularly regarding mood and thought processes. See their article "Affective and Cognitive Characteristics of Depression in 10- and 11-Year-Old Children," *Journal of Personality and Social Psychology* 49 (1985): 194–202. My book *The Depressed Child* also explores how depressed children view the world and others and how they think.

Neal Ryan discusses treatment options for childhood depression, with the particular warning that antidepressant medication has been known to worsen depression symptoms. See "Treatment of Depression in Children and Adolescents," *Lancet* 366 (2005): 933–40. At the same time, David Brent writes that adolescent depression began to decline in the 1990s, perhaps due to the rise of SSRIs. See "Is the Medication Bottle for Pediatric and Adolescent Depression Half-Full or Half-Empty?" *Journal of Adolescent Health* 37 (2005): 431–33.

Lyn Abramson and colleagues discuss the concept of learned helplessness in "Learned Helplessness in Humans — Critique and Reformulation," *Journal of Abnormal Psychology* 87 (1978): 49–74. Scott Compton and colleagues extensively reviewed the existing research literature on the treatment of pediatric anxiety and depression and found that cognitive behavior therapy was the treatment of choice in the majority of controlled studies. See "Cognitive-Behavioral Psychotherapy for Anxiety and Depressive Disorders in Children and Adolescents: An Evidence-Based Medicine Review," *Journal of the American Academy of Child and Adolescent Psychiatry* 43 (2004): 930–59.

Sarah Quakley and colleagues, in a U.K. study, also considered the issue of cognitive behavior therapy with young children. They found that by age seven, most children should be capable of engaging in such therapy. See "Can Children Distinguish Between Thoughts and Behaviours?" *Behavioural and Cognitive Psychotherapy* 31 (2003): 159–68. Similarly, evidence presented by J. H. Flavel and colleagues indicates that younger children are not substantially aware of their own thoughts and may not be candidates for cognitive therapies. See "Development of Children's Awareness of Their Own Thoughts," *Journal of Cognition and Development* 1 (2000): 97–112.

Although the emphasis in the United States has centered heavily on cognitive therapy, Vicky Flory administered parent empathy training to a group of eleven parents in Australia. She found long-term benefits for both child and parent. See "A Novel Clinical Intervention for Severe Childhood Depression and Anxiety," *Clinical Child Psychology and Psychiatry* 9 (2004): 9–23.

Paul Smokowski and K. H. Kopasz studied bullying to determine what type of child is most prone to fall victim to his or her aggressive peers. See "Bullying in School: An Overview of Types, Effects, Family Characteristics, and Intervention Strategies," *Children & Schools* 27 (2005): 101–10. Likewise, Martin Stein and colleagues reported on the complaints of a child who was concealing the fact that he was being bullied. In this case study, the authors show how medical and psychological complaints may be indicators of being bullied. See "Bullying: Concealed by Behavioral and

Somatic Symptoms," *Journal of Developmental & Behavioral Pediatrics* 25 (2004): 347–51.

9. IT SEEMS LIKE EVERYONE LEARNS FASTER THAN ME

Paul McDermott and colleagues examined the risk that having a learning disability creates for developing other problems that may affect behavior and academic performance. Learning disabilities were found to have a wide impact on learning and behavior. See "A Nationwide Epidemiologic Modeling Study of LD: Risk, Protection, and Unintended Impact," *Journal of Learning Disabilities* 39 (2006): 230–51.

Robert Helwig and colleagues examined alternative methods of administering math tests to children known to have learning disabilities. Visual and verbal techniques appeared to improve performance. See "An Oral Versus a Standard Administration of a Large-Scale Mathematics Test," *Journal of Special Education* 36 (2002): 39–47.

Bridget Dalton and colleagues devised an interesting experiment to determine how children with learning disabilities and children without learning disabilities were best able to demonstrate their understanding of a unit on electricity. Children from both groups appeared to do better on a visually oriented test and on a hands-on test, as opposed to a multiple-choice test. Such findings have strong implications for testing procedures. See "Revealing Competence: Fourth-Grade Students With and Without Learning Disabilities Show What They Know on Paper-and-Pencil and Hands-On Performance Assessment," *Learning Disabilities Research & Practice* 10 (1995): 198–214.

Elena Rock and colleagues examined the concomitance of learning disabilities and other psychological disorders. Children with learning disabilities were found to have a greatly increased incidence of social and emotional difficulties in comparison to their peers without learning disabilities. See "The Concomitance of Learning Disabilities and Emotional/Behavioral Disorders: A Conceptual Model," *Journal of Learning Disabilities* 30 (1997): 245–63.

10. BUT I LIKE PLAYING WITH THE YOUNGER KIDS

For further information on maturity, see Jan-Oloy Larsson et al., "An Evaluation of a Short Questionnaire for Parents About Their School-Aged Children's Global Maturity Level," *Child Psychiatry and Human Development* 33 (2002): 59–73. Larsson and colleagues pointed out that immaturity is associated with reduced levels of general knowledge, a childish body appearance, fine-motor difficulties, and difficulties with peers. Symptoms of immaturity might include inattention, impulsivity, poor self-control, and hyperactivity. They also found that these same symptoms can improve later in life due to normal growth or environmental support.

For an examination of the characteristics of children with developmental issues, see Raymond Tervo, "Parent's Reports Predict Their Child's Developmental Problems," *Clinical Pediatrics* 44 (2005): 601–11. Tervo found that symptoms such as eating problems, bowel and bladder problems, clumsiness and fine-motor issues, difficulties with talking and understanding others, and low frequency of playing with others were associated with delayed development. Symptoms related to language in particular increased the odds that a child would experience developmental delays.

For a further explanation of the concept of emotional intelligence, see Daniel Goleman, *Emotional Intelligence: Why It Can Matter More Than IQ* (New York: Bantam Dell, 1995).

11. MY SOCKS AREN'T RIGHT!

For an excellent overview of sensory issues, go to www.webmd.com and enter the search term "sensory processing disorder." Additionally, parents concerned about sensory issues should review Carol Stock Kranowitz's book *The Out-of-Sync Child: Recognizing and Coping with Sensory Processing Disorder* (New York: Penguin, 2005).

Michael Cheng and Jennifer Boggett-Carsjens suggest that clinicians consider that sensory issues may be behind childhood explosions prior to making a diagnosis of bipolar disorder, ADHD, or oppositional defiant disorder. See "Consider Sensory Processing Disorders in the Explosive Child: Case Report and Review," *Canadian Child and Adolescent Psychiatry Review* 14 (2005): 44–48.

Roianne Ahn, along with well-known researchers Lucy Jane Miller and Sharon Milberger, examined the base rates of sensory processing disorders by using survey data. Their study included 703 children. See "Prevalence of Parents' Perceptions of Sensory Processing Disorders Among Kindergarten Children," *American Journal of Occupational Therapy* 58 (2004): 287–93.

12. I'M TIRED!

For information on children's sleep issues, see the National Sleep Foundation's website, www.sleepfoundation.org.

Ronald Chervin is a sleep researcher at the University of Michigan. For his important research on the psychological effects of sleep-disordered breathing, see Chervin et al., "Sleep-Disordered Breathing, Behavior, and Cognition in Children Before and After Adenotonsillectomy," *Pediatrics* 117 (2006): 769–78.

Richard Ferber is a well-known sleep expert. See his book *Solve Your Child's Sleep Problems,* rev. ed. (New York: Simon & Schuster, 2006). This is the first major revision of Ferber's classic on children and sleep, which was first published twenty years ago. This new edition gives updates on the latest research on the nature of sleep in children, the causes of sleep problems, and solutions.

For an important study of the impact of sleep-disordered breathing in children, see J. Gottlieb, "Symptoms of Sleep Disordered Breathing in 5-Year-Old Children Are Associated with Sleepiness and Problem Behavior," *Pediatrics* 112 (2003): 870–77.

13. OCKHAM'S RAZOR: A GUIDING PRINCIPLE FOR DECREASING EXPLOSIONS

Gabriel Masi and colleagues studied a group of ninety-four children and adolescents, finding that approximately a quarter of them also met the diagnostic criteria for ADHD. Other comorbidities also are discussed. See "Comorbidity of Obsessive-Compulsive Disorder and Attention-Deficit/Hyperactivity Disorder in Referred Children and Adolescents," *Comprehensive Psychiatry* 47 (2006): 42–47.

Heather Volk and colleagues evaluated a population of 1,616 subjects, all twins and all known to have ADHD. High rates of comorbid oppositional defiant disorder/conduct disorder and depression were found. See "A Systematic Evaluation of ADHD and Comorbid Psychopathology in a Population-Based Twin Sample," *Journal of the American Academy of Child and Adolescent Psychiatry* 44 (2005): 768–75.

Elena Rock and colleagues, reviewed in the chapter 9 notes, found strong connections between learning disabilities and other forms of behavioral and emotional difficulties. See "The Concomitance of Learning Disabilities and Emotional/Behavioral Disorders: A Conceptual Model," *Journal of Learning Disabilities* 30 (1997): 245–63.

Alan Kazdin and Moira Whitley tested the complexity hypothesis on a group of 183 children between the ages of three and fourteen. Comorbidity of symptoms was not associated with treatment outcome, as would be expected by the complexity hypothesis. See "Comorbidity, Case Complexity, and Effects of Evidence-Based Treatment for Children Referred for Disruptive Behavior," *Journal of Consulting and Clinical Psychology* 74 (2006): 455–67.

INDEX